— THE —
CLUTTER-FREE
HOME

KATHI LIPP

HARVEST HOUSE PUBLISHERS
EUGENE, OREGON

Cover design by Emily Weigel Design

Cover photo © Photographee.eu/shutterstock

Published in association with Books & Such Literary Management, 52 Mission Circle, Suite 122, PMB 170, Santa Rosa, CA 95409-5370, www.booksandsuch.com.

Portions of the chapter "Use It Up, Wear It Out, Make It Do, or Do Without" appear in *Clutter Free* © 2015 by Kathi Lipp.

The Clutter-Free Home
Copyright © 2020 by Kathi Lipp
Published by Harvest House Publishers
Eugene, Oregon 97408
www.harvesthousepublishers.com

ISBN 978-0-7369-7698-5 (pbk.)
ISBN 978-0-7369-7699-2 (eBook)

Library of Congress Cataloging-in-Publication Data

Names: Lipp, Kathi, author.
Title: The clutter-free home : making room for your life / Kathi Lipp.
Description: Eugene : Harvest House Publishers, 2020.
Identifiers: LCCN 2019032738 (print) | LCCN 2019032739 (ebook) | ISBN 9780736976985 (paperback) | ISBN 9780736976992 (ebook)
Subjects: LCSH: Storage in the home. | Orderliness. | House cleaning.
Classification: LCC TX309 .L55455 2020 (print) | LCC TX309 (ebook) | DDC 648/.8--dc23
LC record available at https://lccn.loc.gov/2019032738
LC ebook record available at https://lccn.loc.gov/2019032739

Printed in the United States of America

19 20 21 22 23 24 25 26 27 / BP-SK / 10 9 8 7 6 5 4 3 2 1

To Tonya Kubo
You found freedom through *Clutter Free*,
and you share hope every day with others
who desperately need freedom.
You have loved our Clutter Free
Academy community well.
You have mercy for those who
are still on the path.
I am so grateful for you and the
life-giving work you do for so many.

CONTENTS

At Peace with Your Home 7

Understanding Clutter 15

The Ten Principles of a Clutter-Free Home 17

PART 1—THE STEPS

Step 1: Dedicate 25

Step 2: Decide 31

Step 3: Declutter 39

Step 4: Do Your Thing 57

PART 2—THE SPACES

The Kitchen 69

The Living Room 85

The Bedroom 99

The Bathroom 117

The Office 137

The Other Space 159

Living Clutter Free with Kids 177

Use It Up, Wear It Out, Make It Do, or Do Without . . . 181

A Final Word 197

Notes 199

AT PEACE WITH YOUR HOME

wanted to just give up.

I was so tired. Tired of living in chaos. Tired of feeling like I needed to remodel the house every time I wanted to clean it.

Making life run with a husband and four kids took so much *stuff*, and I had no place to put it. I felt helpless, unable to change. So this was the life we were doomed to: controlled and not-so-controlled chaos.

Then I went to my friend Deb's house.

Deb was the mom of five kids and lived in a house with even fewer square feet than mine. We were at her house to get ready for a PTA project, and I couldn't believe her place when I walked in. The home wasn't spotless or fussy, but it was totally her.

When our time together wound down, after we'd had such a great afternoon, I told her (as I would tell any good friend), "Next time, you don't have to clean house for me." That is my ultimate "obviously we are going to be amazing friends" card.

She said offhandedly, "Oh, I didn't. No worries." And after the next few meetings at her home (I wasn't letting her into *my* house), I soon discovered why.

Deb had no clutter.

It wasn't that the house was perfect—there were dishes in the sink and backpacks on the table—or that the furniture was fancy. In fact, I noticed around visit number three that some of it didn't even match. But there was no clutter: no piles of papers waiting to be sorted, no extra toys waiting to be put away, no collection of plastic cups from local eateries sitting on the counters. Everything had a place and a use.

And that's when my life took a turn. I wanted to grow up to be Deb.

Chances are, if you picked up this book, you've had your own "Deb" moment. Maybe you doubt you can ever get free of the clutter. Maybe you've tried to declutter before, but your efforts were soon thwarted by more papers, toys, and clothes covering every flat surface. You might have even thought, *Why bother? It's a never-ending battle.*

Since that first day at Deb's house, I've figured out a way not only to get rid of the clutter (without becoming a minimalist), but to make sure my home stays decluttered. And let me tell you: If I can do it, then you can too. I promise.

This is my wish for you:

I want you to have a home that stays decluttered.

I want you to feel at peace when you walk into your home.

I want you to have a home that nourishes you and the people you love.

THE HABIT OF *NO*

We tend to think that we are the only ones on our block who are in a battle with clutter. But statistics show that 54 percent of us deal with clutter in a big way in our homes.[1] In other words, most of us (*most!*) feel that clutter is a big stressor on our lives. That's because our desires and habits are diametrically opposed. We desire simplicity and rest. We desire organized minds and calendars. We desire harmony. But we haven't built the daily habits that will make those desires a reality.

I have a few big desires—a few big *yeses*—in my life. I want to have a home that I love and feel completely at ease in. I want to have enough money to travel, to give to causes I believe in, and, eventually, to have a dignified retirement. I want to spend time on work I believe in and causes I care about.

It takes a thousand little *nos* to get to your one big *yes*. And in this book, I'm going to make suggestions for a thousand *nos*. Some of these, especially if you are a clutter keeper, are going to seem ridiculous. *Use up that shower gel I've been hanging on to for a year? It's not going to hurt anyone if I keep one bottle.* No, it won't. But the problem is, it's not just one bottle. There are a thousand decisions like that in each of our homes, and if you want to develop the mind of a clutter flinger, you've got to give yourself some hard-and-fast rules. You have to be diligent to keep the clutter from creeping in.

So as you read through this book, if you are struck by the thought, *Oh brother, that small change can't make a difference*, know that you are right—but also realize that a thousand small tweaks combined can make a huge difference.

THE HABITS OF CLUTTER KEEPERS VS. CLUTTER FLINGERS

Clutter Keepers: *I'll leave this out in case I want to come back to it later.*

Clutter Flingers: *I'll put this away now.*

THE PURPOSE OF YOUR HOME

We've all been asked if we wanted a tour of someone's house. (I have never in my life offered a tour of my house to anyone. Ever.) And the thing that always blows me away is the kids' bathroom. It's pristine. Even with four children, the kids' bathroom looks like it's in one of those model homes. Please. Four kids? A bathroom in which you could perform minor surgery? You know your host was getting busy with some Clorox wipes three minutes before you arrived.

And that's fine. But when did it become important to pretend that the only people who live in your house are Nate Berkus and Mr. Clean? I want you to have a home that is beautiful (and this book is going to go a long way in getting you there), but I want it to be beautiful because you live in it—not because someone else might see it.

I want for your home what I want for mine: for it to be clean enough that you and others feel comfortable in the space. But I also want the space to be a reflection of you. What you love, what you do, what is important to you. Because here is what I know for sure: The better your home is for you, the better you are for the world.

We're not aiming for Pinterest-perfect here. The goal as you begin this journey is to create a home where you can spend peaceful time with your family and host company without losing your mind.

So much marketing is designed to make us dissatisfied with our homes. When I look at the HGTV channel, the Target ads, the magazines, I think about how shallow home decorating can be. We think, *If I could finally replace my ratty kitchen rugs, then I'd love my home.* We spend all our money and effort to get a specific look without spending the time to understand how our surroundings make us feel.

I get exhausted when I think about all the ways I'm *supposed* to make my home look and feel to impress others. But when I think about using my home for rest and restoration and how that helps me be in the world, with my people, and with God, I think to myself, *Let me go fluff that pillow and declutter that drawer.*

◇◇◇◇◇◇◇◇◇◇◇◇◇◇◇◇◇

Your home should be beautiful
because you live in it—not
because someone else might see it.

◇◇◇◇◇◇◇◇◇◇◇◇◇◇◇◇◇

First, we'll look at some general principles, and then I'll help you apply them step by step. This book is a room-by-room guide to decluttering, reclaiming, and celebrating every space of your home. And just so you know who you're dealing with here, I'm not preaching minimalism, scarcity, and living without. That is not my jam. I want to encourage you to get purposeful about the place you live in and the possessions you live with. You see, having a clutter-free home doesn't mean doing without. It's about doing life *with* those things you use and love.

In order for us to get purposeful about our homes, we'll take four specific steps:

1. dedicate
2. decide
3. declutter
4. do your thing

Why do I want you to go in this order? Because I'm guessing that, like me, you've gotten this wrong. A lot. You've decided that you want to freshen up a room, so the first thing you do is head to T.J. Maxx or the Joanna Gaines section of Target and buy a couple of cute items to give your room a new look. The problem is, if you've bought the cute before you've decluttered, that cute will just get lost in the clutter. (Have you ever noticed that the letters for *cute* are all contained in *clutter*? Mind blowing, right? It's like all that cute is begging us, "Don't let me get lost in the clutter!")

Or you go and buy that cute decoration, but you haven't spent any time deciding what that room should feel like, and now the cute is no longer cute. Worse, it's actually annoying you. You keep having to move it around, because it—like everything else in the room—just doesn't work. So I want you to take some time, pull back, and really, really think through each room of your house.

Don't worry—you won't have to figure out these steps on your own. In the next few chapters, we'll work through each of them together. But I want you to remember the four steps and commit them (and their order) to memory. Because you will be using them. A lot.

IT'S NOT THE NUMBER OF ROOMS

I don't know your home. I'm sitting here in San Jose, California, writing a book. I haven't been to your house. (Hey, is there a reason you haven't invited me over yet? Oh—that's right...the clutter.)

But one thing I already know about where you live—it's nothing like where I live. You probably don't have a spot on the stairs where your son, in a fit of hormonal rage, left a dent that has marked the passing of time. And I'm guessing you don't have a saggy third cushion on your couch that you have strategically propped up with a hidden beach towel to make springier. And you for sure don't have a purple velvet armchair with a turquoise ottoman in your office, for which you are still in search of the perfect pillow to pull it all together...

And I'm also guessing that my house, when it comes to size, is somewhere in the middle of all my readers' homes. I live in a town house that is 1,441 square feet. It's an awesome size for us now. It didn't feel so awesome when Roger and I first got married and had four kids, but I digress. Maybe you live in a much smaller space. Or maybe you live in a much bigger space. But hear me and hear me well: I have lived in every house size and situation known to man. And I've kept that fact (and you) in mind while I've been writing this book. Because no matter how many or few rooms we have, we each have our lives to lead—and those lives require stuff. And stuff? It takes up space.

To my friends with larger homes...

Since publishing *Clutter Free*, in which I talked about how we didn't need a mountain house because we had so many friends with homes they were willing to lend us, well...we bought a mountain house.

A big mountain house. (It's a long story—a God story. But that's another book.)

Zillow says the home is 2,500 square feet, but since buying it, we've realized that it has two unpermitted areas that were built on later, so it's more like 3,000 square feet. And let me tell you, it would be the easiest house in the world to fill up with clutter. And that clutter would be so easy to hide. There are numerous cabinets, drawers, and shelves, in addition to a barn, a garage, an attic, and even a woodshed. Oh, the clutter that could be contained. *Swoon...* (That's a bit of my pre-*Clutter Free* self peeking out.)

And then, on the other hand, there are a lot of rooms. When it comes to the thought of dedicating, deciding, decluttering, and then doing my thing in all those rooms—four bedrooms, three living spaces, two storage areas, plus the kitchen and office and three bathrooms—it feels like a lot. Like a *lot* a lot.

If you are in a similar situation, do not be overwhelmed by the number of rooms you're facing. (Just breathe deeply into a bag.) It will take as long as it takes, but there's one thing I can assure you of: When you stick with it, the job will get done. The process may not go as quickly as it does for your friends with smaller houses, but it will happen. Take your time. For example, get one of the bedrooms 60 percent decluttered before moving on to the next bedroom. You will still need to maintain all the bedrooms and work on them, and it will take longer, but eventually, it will all be clutter free.

And someday, you may even have some empty drawers. Think about that! Glory be…

To my friends with smaller homes...

My first time living on my own was as a missionary in Japan. My entire apartment had one interior door. (And that wasn't even to the toilet. The toilet was outside on my balcony.)

Your first (or fifth) home may also be of the postage-stamp variety. But that doesn't mean that it will automatically be clutter free. In fact, it can be downright amazing how much stuff we as humans can stuff into a small space.

Even if you don't have six different *rooms* in your home, you do have *spaces* for cooking, living, sleeping, hygiene, working, and storage. (That is, the kitchen, living room, bedroom, bathroom, office, and garage.) In my tiny apartment in Japan, I had a kitchenette that was one space in the apartment. My bedroom and living room were the same space since I packed up my futon each morning (okay, most mornings) and put it in my closet. I actually had two bathrooms (one inside, one on the balcony), and my office area was a desk in my living room. I didn't really have a storage space, but I did have a laundry area—also on the balcony.

With the rooms being multipurpose, it was even more important to keep my space clutter free. There is nothing worse than having to move piles of junk to set up your bed when all you want to do late at night is crawl into it.

Whether you live in a tiny house or something more akin to a mansion, clutter is the enemy. I want you to take back your house and actually "right-size" your possessions so that you can reclaim the space, time, energy, and money that clutter has been stealing from you all these years. That way you can stop worrying about how big your house is and love the house you have.

WAY STATION

For too long I lived my life thinking that the only purpose of my house was to let me redress and refuel so I could go back into the world. I would only go grocery shopping when I was absolutely out of food (and out of money to buy fast food). I would only do the laundry when I was out of clean underwear. My house was just a place where I could stop on the way to other, more important things. But as I've gotten older (and hopefully, a tiny bit wiser), I've realized that the good stuff—the ministry, the healing, the love and connection—happens as much within the four walls of my home as it does outside them.

The key? We have to let people in. And in order to let people in, we need to be at peace with the home we have.

So let's get started.

⟨⟨◇◇⟩⟩✕✕⟨⟨◇◇⟩⟩✕✕⟨⟨◇◇

The better your home is for you,
the better you are for the world.

⟩✕✕⟨⟨◇◇⟩⟩✕✕⟨⟨◇◇⟩⟩✕✕

UNDERSTANDING CLUTTER

What exactly is clutter? Let's take a moment to define it. When I talk to people about clutter, I give them three questions to help them determine if a specific item is clutter:

1. Do you love it?

2. Do you use it?

3. Would you buy it again?

If you can answer a strong *yes* to any of these three questions, then it's not clutter. (But if the item you "love" is stored in a box in your garage, I'm going to question your love.)

However, if you only feel so-so on one question, it's time to consider giving up that item. Sometimes you have to build up to the kind of brave that lets you get rid of things you might need someday…maybe. Don't worry—if you can't give it up the first time you ask yourself the three questions, you will start to get so excited about your home becoming decluttered that you'll eventually want to give it all away. I promise you'll find a declutter-y place in the middle. (Somewhere between *minimalist* and *hoarder*.)

Here are some examples of clutter you can get rid of right now, guilt free:

- the 11 color-coordinated boxes full of old issues of *Real Simple* you didn't even read when they were new
- the photos from the office Christmas party in 1998 showcasing past coworkers you no longer speak to (They know what they did…)
- the bag of clothes you've been meaning to run to Goodwill for six weeks now but have started to root through when laundry piles up
- the box of taco shells older than your firstborn
- anything on a floppy disk

I promise, you can do this. Those things you've held on to out of fear (just in case you need them someday) will eventually leave your house without your giving them a second glance.

THE TEN PRINCIPLES OF A CLUTTER-FREE HOME

1. Make clutter management a daily habit.

Clutter is never "one and done." It's like laundry. You're never done with laundry (unless you decide to step out into a wild new lifestyle choice and become a nudist), because while you are folding and putting away the last of the laundry from the pile, you are still wearing clothes that need to go into that laundry pile.

It's the same with clutter. There is the real clutter we need to get out of our homes (magazines we will never read again, crafts we have outgrown, sixth grade spelling bee awards), and then there is the clutter of everyday life (the schoolwork, the mail, the work project, etc.) that must be managed. No, schoolwork isn't clutter...until it's left on the breakfast bar overnight and then, *poof:* real life becomes clutter.

So just as you will never be done with laundry, you will never be done with decluttering.

And that's okay. Because as much as I want you to get rid of real clutter, I want you to be able to manage real life. To know where the mail goes when it enters your house. To know where your family will put their shoes when they kick them off. Clutter will enter your life, but it doesn't have to take over your life.

2. Designate a place for everything.

I think 20 percent of our clutter comes from the fact that we have things we need, but we don't have a designated place to put them. We know we *should* know where they go, but we haven't taken the time to truly think through the placement and assign the items a spot.

Any time you have that vague feeling of *I know I need to keep this, but I don't know where to put it, so I'll put it here for now*...stop. Make a decision, even if it's wrong. You can fix it later. I promise you—this will greatly reduce your clutter instantly.

3. Don't put it aside. Put it away.

I am an optimistic girl. I truly believe life is only going to get better. I believe I will have more time later on to do things like cleaning up the kitchen, hanging up my coat, and going through the stuff stored in the garage. And so I have spent most of my life thinking, *I'll get to that later—when I have more time.*

Yeah...that "more time" rarely shows up. I could spend hours every week doing a massive cleanup. But if I put items away as I use them instead of just tossing them aside, I don't have to spend all my free time cleaning up after myself.

I actually say to myself, "Kathi, don't put it aside. Put it away!" as I'm walking through the house. I don't say it in a *tsk tsk* manner. I use it as a gentle reminder that if I want a clutter-free home, putting things away is one of the main practices I need to ingrain in my mind and life.

4. Stop being reactive and start being proactive.

Reactive decluttering looks like this: *Oh no, my mother-in-law is coming over! I've got to deal with all this junk!* (Most likely, instead of decluttering, you are actually doing one of my most famous moves— the "stash and dash," where instead of getting rid of clutter, you just move it around.) But proactive decluttering looks like this: *I would love for this space to have less clutter. I'm setting my alarm for 15 minutes, and I'll see how much I can clear up in that time.*

5. Don't argue over stuff. Negotiate space.

The number-one question I get is "What do I do about my
_____'s stuff?" (Usually that blank is filled by *husband*, but occasionally I see *wife, kid, grown child*, or *parent*.) People who ask that question want me to tell them that they have every right to be upset about someone else's clutter. I've heard stories of people pitching their husband's "junk" and wanting me to give my *Clutter Free* stamp of approval.

Yeah, that's not going to happen. I tell people, "I have the answer, but you won't like it." The only tactic that I've ever seen work is to stop arguing about stuff and start agreeing on space.

While your relatives may never be convinced that they can get rid of their track shoes from high school (even if high school was during a Bush presidency), most people can understand the need for equal space. So while arguing over an old guitar (the one nobody has played since attempting "Smoke on the Water" in the store) will get you nowhere, agreeing that everyone keeps their own stuff in one extra closet or on one rack in the garage can make a real difference for two reasons. First, it's not enough space to hold "all my stuff." It's a finite, predetermined amount of space that the stuff *has* to fit into. Second, you can take yourself out of the argument. When you and your loved one agree on the space, the space itself—not you—is making the demands and forcing decisions.

But this only works if you are taking a hard look at your own clutter and showing your loved one that you are also willing to make the hard but necessary decisions. It is easy to spot someone else's obvious clutter yet tell ourselves a story that justifies our own. Take out that clutter log in your own eye before pointing out your loved one's clutter speck.

6. Don't use storage as a way to delay decisions.

Yep—this one is hard to hear. Unless it is "active storage" (such as Christmas decorations, gardening supplies, etc.), most of what we store is stuff we don't want to make decisions about. Usually it includes items we feel are too important to get rid of but not important enough to have in our homes. We can't bear the thought of regretting letting it go, so instead, we delay the decision by putting it in a tub and opening that tub every year when we finally clean out the garage, basement, or attic. But all we end up doing is lifting the lid, looking at the item, feeling a pang of guilt, and putting it back in the box for another year.

7. Once you diagnose the clutter, you can dispense with it.

We hold on to clutter for one of three reasons—or a combination thereof.

- Fear: *But I might need it someday.*
- Guilt: *But _____ gave it to me.*
- Shame: *But I spent so much money on it.*

Once you figure out why you're holding on to the clutter—the real, gut reaction to that item and why you can't get rid of it—it becomes easier to reason with yourself and finally get rid of what you don't need.

8. Things are not relationships.

This may be one of the hardest principles for us to come to grips with as a society. We have been convinced that if we love someone, we hold on to everything that person ever gave us, ever.

Yes, I love it when I give a gift and the recipient loves it. But I would hate to think that anyone is keeping gifts around to prove we have a good relationship. My kids are the perfect example. If I buy them something and it's not a good fit (for their size, their home, or their life), none of them are shy about asking for the receipt. And while I hate that I missed the mark, I'm glad they are not just taking something to be polite.

I don't have that kind of relationship with everyone, so there are times when, even though I'm grateful that someone thought of me, a gift goes straight to the donation center or to someone else who can use it. There is nothing honoring about keeping an unused gift in the garage for three years before donating it.

We can also convince ourselves that if we love someone who has passed, we need to keep every sentimental item as a shrine to prove our love for them.

Ridiculous.

"Things are not relationships" is the mantra I've had to use when deciding what to do about items from my late dad. I've decided to keep the things that bring back great memories and let the rest go. There were hundreds of items that reminded me of him, but those items are not holding the memories. I am.

9. Just-in-case thinking is impoverished thinking.

If I'm holding on to old shoes I don't like and wouldn't wear right now because they pinch, but I'm going to keep them "just in case," I've got a pretty pessimistic view of the world. That attitude says...

- *I believe my situation is going to get worse, not better.*
- *I don't trust myself to provide what I need in the future.*
- *I don't trust God to provide what I need in the future.*

If I lose my job, if financial disaster hits, I'm guessing there is no scenario where I'll be wearing shoes that pinch. I would rather resole the shoes I currently wear and love than wear shoes that make me miserable. There is not one single reason for me to hold on to shoes I don't wear except for extreme, impoverished thinking, and that is no way to think—or live.

10. You deserve peace in your home.

Maybe you've had a clutter problem your whole life. Maybe you've had a hard time keeping a room clean and clutter free, much less an entire home. Maybe, deep down, you don't believe you deserve a nice place to live. I'm not talking about a fancy or expensive space; I'm talking clean, neat, and peaceful.

Let me say this: We all deserve a peaceful place where we can rest our heads at night.

For most of my life, I've lived with hand-me-down dressers and furniture purchased in the Reagan era. But only in the last decade have I come to realize that imperfect furniture doesn't mean I can't have my dream home.

Your dream house doesn't need to include a specific couch or the table you've been looking at online for years. It needs to have a couch without Mount Fold-Me on it and a table that is clear of clutter and set with love.

— PART 1 —

THE STEPS

Step 1

DEDICATE

We all do better with a purpose. Little kids like to know that they are helping. (Even if their "helping" will cause you 25 minutes of cleanup later on.) Most adults I know would much rather be part of the action than sitting on the sidelines, waiting for the work to be done. Think about how uncomfortable you are at a gathering if you ask what you can do and the hostess says, "Oh, just relax." You stand there awkwardly wishing you had some romaine to chop.

Your room is the same: It's dying to have a purpose. And that is what this first step is all about. The clutter has taken control, and you need to determine the room's purpose before you can take back control. In this step, you are going to figure out exactly how you use each room and then dedicate the room to that purpose.

DRIFT

I'm guessing one of the main reasons for your clutter frustrations is *drift*. Items that are supposed to be in another room have drifted into this room.

Hey, it happens. I'm looking at my kitchen now. I opened an

Amazon box yesterday, and there sits my bottle of Big Sexy Hair. And it would be fine, if it were just that. But I also got a package from a friend containing a book, a jar of Hershey's Kisses, and some more fun items. And then there are some books I need to read for work. And the mail. Any of these items on their own? Not a problem. But gather them together and give it a little time? This becomes a mess too overwhelming to deal with.

THE TOP 5 USES FOR MY KITCHEN

1. cooking

2. eating

3. connecting

4. working

5. storing food

One of the reasons we get into cluttered situations (and homes) is that we haven't dedicated our spaces to their intended purposes. We find our kids' homework in the living room, recipes in the office, and clothes in the kitchen or, more frighteningly, the fridge (true story).

Look at the room you are in right now. What are the top five intended uses for that space? Here is an example:

Like almost every room in my home, the kitchen is a multipurpose room. I use it for a variety of tasks. But the heart of the room is found in those five purposes.

As you start to reshape your room into the space you want it to be, keep your top-five purposes in mind. (I write them on a Post-it so I can remember them when I'm in that room.) If you come across something in the room that doesn't fit the purpose of the space or just doesn't feel right there, it's time to either move the item back where it belongs or give it away.

IT'S A SIGN

One tool I've found super helpful when it comes to dedicating each room is to display a quotation, Bible verse, or some kind of sign that focuses my family as we use the space. It doesn't have to be a big sign. It could be as simple as a piece of paper inside a cabinet door. The important part is that you know it's there as a reminder of how you've dedicated the space.

For our kitchen, we ordered a big wooden sign from a designer on Etsy that says, "The Lipp-Smackin' Café—Sit Long, Talk Much." That sign perfectly encapsulates the feeling I want myself and my loved ones to have as we work, eat, and connect in our kitchen.

In our bedroom, we have a quote from C.S. Lewis's book *The Last Battle*: "Now at last they were beginning Chapter One of the Great Story which no one on earth has read: which goes on forever: in which every chapter is better than the one before."[2] I chose this for our bedroom since I want Roger and I to always work on making our current chapter better than the one before.

And here is the quote from J.R.R. Tolkien's *The Fellowship of the Ring* that we use for our living room, which we have specifically designed to be a gathering space: "'A perfect house, whether you like food or sleep or story-telling or singing, or just sitting and thinking best, or a pleasant mixture of them all.' Merely to be there was a cure for weariness, fear, and sadness."[3]

You can also find sign ideas from song lyrics and lines from poetry. Whatever you choose, make sure it's personal and meaningful to you and your family. Having something tangible to remind you of the purpose of your room makes it easier to identify what doesn't belong there. Dedicating a room is pre-decluttering.

MY [UN]CLUTTERED LIFE

— Holly —

Where are my keys?

Where's your homework?

I can't find...anything!

Before I was introduced to Kathi and her decluttering methods, my life was a mess. I had no idea where anything was. The thought of someone coming to my house terrified me, because I didn't want anyone to see how I lived. My mom even told people that I was a great mom— and that's why my house was always a mess. Even my best friend told me her husband didn't know how I could live in that mess.

I had systems. Oh, I've tried them all. I tossed and stuffed and hid things. I spent more money than I care to think about on one system or another, and I spent countless hours trying to organize my possessions. If company was coming, I even had a system to prepare for that: I would collect everything in baskets and stuff it beside my bed where no one would see.

And then I learned one important lesson: You can't organize clutter. So why was I keeping so much stuff? I honestly didn't know. I just knew I couldn't give it away.

Since I've learned Kathi's clutter-free method, I now know I don't have to keep everything anymore. I know the reason I was keeping things and have overcome my fear, guilt, and shame. I can find what I need, and I don't buy duplicates because I know what I have and where each item is. I am using routines to keep the house clean so I have time to spend with my family instead of having to clear a place on the table for dinner. I have also learned that I was using shopping to make myself feel better in hard situations.

As I got rid of more and more things, God showed me other areas of clutter. I have not only strived to declutter the visible (my home, office, and other spaces), but I am now decluttering my heart and mind. That "friend" who shared her husband's thoughts about my messy house? She is no longer in my life. I now have healthy relationships with people who care about me and build me up. I am finishing projects and have been able to bless others with my time. I'm not wasting that time caring for things that are not important to me.

In short, I am becoming the person God has called me to be because I am no longer a slave to what doesn't matter.

DECIDE

One of my favorite blogs of all time is *Thistlewood Farms* (www.thistlewoodfarms.com). You know it's one of my favorites because it goes to my main inbox instead of the other email address I use to subscribe to everything else—like store coupons and antivirus updates. That's true love. KariAnne Wood, the author behind the blog, shows pictures of her amazing house and all the projects she does. It's so inspiring and amazing. And there are days when it just makes my heart glad.

And then there are days when it completely bums me out.

When I spend time looking at KariAnne's blog—or any blog, magazine, HGTV show, or Pinterest board showcasing someone's amazingly decorated house—I would love to say that my first thought is one of admiration. But, to be honest, it's often one of comparison. I compare my living room to the one on the blog. *Why can't my room look like that? Why does everyone get to have a beautiful house besides me? Why can't decorating come naturally to me?*

And then I learned the deep, dark secret of designers everywhere: Whereas creating a cute room comes more naturally to some than others, most of the magic comes from actually thinking through a room. Designers move items around, try different pillows, create color palettes, and more. (It's like they have this secret society where they exchange fringe tips and painted weathered-wood sealing techniques, and they didn't bother to invite the rest of us. Rude.)

I am the ultimate sucker for a cute throw pillow, a perfect piece of framed art, or a great chair. I used to buy those things, bring them home, and then realize they weren't really perfect. They were just bright, shiny objects I wanted and had no place to put. But taking those items back to the store felt like too much trouble, and garage sales don't exactly accept returns. So instead of getting rid of those items, I kept them. And nothing—and I mean nothing—in my house made sense, felt cute, or worked together.

Even before decluttering, you need to make some decisions about each room (or space) in your home. Either you decide how you want the room to feel, or the room will decide for you. Often, the difference between someone with a beautiful home and someone who struggles with clutter is that the BH (Beautiful Home) person has given their house a great deal of thought and made decisions *before* going to Target or a garage sale. I want CH (Cluttered Home) people to start getting intentional about how their home functions and feels.

There's a question we need to ask ourselves before we declutter (or buy that cute end table that is actually just a tree stump): *How do I want to feel when I walk into the room each day?* Here's how I answered that for my kitchen:

1. clean

2. comfortable

3. creative

4. cozy

5. connected

(Your words don't need to be alliterative, but boy, it's a bonus if they are!)

How will you experience those feelings you want the room to evoke? With your five senses. Deciding what to do with a room with those senses in mind will help you create the feelings you want. Let's just take one of the senses—sight—and break it down for the kitchen.

SIGHT

What do I want to *see* as I walk into the kitchen each morning? Looking at the five ways I want my kitchen to feel, I had to make some decisions.

Clean

When I walk into the kitchen first thing in the morning, the last thing I want to see is chaos. First, I keep my kitchen clean by having white walls. White says "clean" to me. Second, I keep as much stuff off the counters as possible to give the space an uncluttered look. Third, every night I clean off the counters, kitchen table, and butcher block and do dishes so I'm greeted by a clean kitchen in the morning.

This effort isn't easy to maintain, so I have taken a three-pronged approach to cleaning my kitchen.

1. I see it as a team effort. Roger hates cleaning the kitchen. I hate doing dishes. So he does the dishes while I clean the kitchen. This is what true, everlasting love looks like.

2. I frame it in a new way. Instead of thinking of kitchen duty as cleaning up from the mess of making dinner, I think about it as taking care of my future self. I think about how much tomorrow-morning Kathi (and Roger) will love coming down to a clean kitchen instead of feeling defeat first thing in the morning. This makes me want to clean all the things.

3. I listen to something awesome. I put on the news or an audiobook or some Eagles music and actually enjoy not being at a computer (my day job), but rather getting to stand up and move around and listen to something I love. I have one audiobook going at a time that is only for while I'm cleaning. This makes me want to earn the right to put it on and listen. (My current book is *Educated* by Tara Westover, and I can't wait to clean the grout so I can get to the next chapter.)

Comfortable

When we replaced our 25-year-old secondhand kitchen table, we got a big farm table that practically begs you to sit down and stay a while. If a piece of wood furniture can be considered comfy, this is that piece of furniture.

I want to encourage my guests and family to be comfortable. I want them to have the drink they want, a snack that makes them happy, and a chair they can sit in. There is not one thing in my kitchen that could be considered "fussy." No precious china, no thin glass that has to be cared for, and nothing that has to be hand-washed. Every inch of that room needs to be livable.

Creative

This space is where I love to create meals, write, and collaborate with other people. I love the newly white walls, the giant table, and the massive (five feet tall) clock. There is a whole piece of furniture dedicated to making coffee (and all the Torani flavors that go with a proper cup of coffee). I know what it takes for me and my people to be creative. Coffee is critical.

Cozy

I love studying the idea of *hygge*, the Danish art of making a space cozy. When I think "cozy," I think "welcoming." What could I see in my kitchen that would make me want to sit down and stay a while?

In the fall and winter, it's a cozy blanket on the back of a kitchen chair and a tray of mugs on the table, ready for coffee and cocoa. In the spring and summer, it's fresh flowers on the kitchen table and glasses for iced tea. The little, non-cluttered touches make my family and guests feel loved.

Connected

Our sign "Sit Long, Talk Much" says it all. That is the goal of our space—not just to feed our faces (which is also critical), but to feed our spirits with great conversation and connection.

THE OTHER SENSES

Beyond sight, let's explore the other senses to see how they can create the feelings you want each room to give.

Smell. Each room can have a signature scent. For my kitchen, it's Mrs. Meyer's lemon verbena dish soap, hand soap, and lotion—plus coffee brewing in the morning.

Taste. Yes, the kitchen is all about taste. How can you get more of the taste you want into your space? Be intentional. Provide a selection of teas for your guests. Set up your coffee for the morning before you go to bed. Plan meals—because the best way to be happy when you walk into your kitchen is to know what you're having for dinner.

When I'm baking, I will make a couple batches of muffin batter, spray a muffin pan with oil, fill the cups, and freeze them to create something I call "muffin pucks." When I want to have a hot breakfast the next morning, I pull out a couple of pucks, put them in a small four-cup muffin pan, and let them defrost overnight. The next morning, I stick the pan in the toaster oven and have fresh-from-the-oven muffins.

Touch. Just because everyone else on the planet has lost their minds over microfiber towels does not mean that you need to own them. (They give my husband and me the heebie-jeebies.) Find your own favorite towel and rock on.

Sound. What can I hear that will help the kitchen feel clean, comfortable, creative, cozy, and connectional? I need an Amazon Echo and a quiet dishwasher. Find the sounds that help you create your own favorite feelings.

There will be space in part 2 for you to determine how you want each of your rooms to feel. Then you can use your five senses to figure out how to achieve that feel. No more "accidental" rooms! Every room in your home will be a room created and curated on purpose.

ZONES

Creating a room's zones is all about understanding what activities go on in that room and organizing and staging the room accordingly.

When I ask you to create zones in part 2, think through how you and your people actually use that space. I like to think about a doctor's office. The office manager doesn't keep the blood-testing equipment next to the patient files. (If they do, I would highly suggest you switch doctors.) Make your room make sense.

◇◇◇✕✕✕◇◇◇◇✕✕✕◇◇◇◇◇◇

Either you decide how you want the room
to feel, or the room will decide for you.

✕✕◇◇◇◇✕✕✕◇◇◇◇✕✕✕◇

FROM FAILURE TO FREEDOM

— Cathy —

At 63, I would love to tell you self-criticism goes away with age—but it doesn't. Not with a delayed diagnosis of ADHD, not with infinite books and organizing systems, not with therapy, not through avoiding becoming a hoarder like my mother or sister. No, the self-loathing remained. I was a lost cause. I had given up.

Because my children are grown and gone, I could fake the cleanliness of the "public rooms" in my house by using my go-to "stash and dash" method. Nonetheless, I felt like a failure.

And then I discovered Kathi Lipp and Cheri Gregory talking about their book *Overwhelmed*. I started listening to *The Clutter Free Academy* podcast, and I realized that shame and self-loathing cannot produce decluttering success. There is no magic, mystical way to get organized. Becoming clutter free is not a how-to process in 500 "easy" steps. This is not a "delve into your past to blame others for your clutter" method.

Change comes first through understanding that we're not alone. Through the Clutter Free Academy (which is "the kindest corner of the internet"—supporting, caring, realistic, and practical), I've found a family of like-minded people in the same boat as me. And I've learned how to stop my life-long negative self-talk. Even though I still have my "hot mess" areas, I believe that by the end of the year every area in my home will be decluttered. Best of all, I will finally be free to do and be everything God wants me to do and be.

Step 3

DECLUTTER

Dedicating each room to a purpose and deciding how it should function makes decluttering that much easier. Nothing should stay unless it serves the purpose of that room. So now it's time to declutter.

We cluttered people are not known for our moderation. As someone who once had thirteen bookcases (including one in the bathroom), let's just say that extreme living was pretty much my life for many, many years. My household's routine was to live like rock stars during the week, trashing rooms like housekeeping and an insurance rider would take care of the damage, and then spend all weekend trying to get our home into model-house mode—until Monday came, and we started the routine all over again.

Like I said, moderation is not my jam.

That is, until I found a better way. I wondered, *What if I actually stay on top of the cleaning and decluttering on an almost daily basis? Then I'd have at least part of the weekend to hang out with my husband and kids, and I'd avoid all the yelling that accompanies anger cleaning.*

Decluttering is not "one and done." It's a routine you establish that brings peace of mind for the rest of your life. There are two parts to my decluttering routine:

1. Daily declutter: Every day, you will spend 15 minutes decluttering an assigned room in your house.

2. Deep declutter: Each week, you will spend 60 minutes doing a deep declutter of one room until it is mostly decluttered.

See? Not so overwhelming, right? You can do this. Let's break each step down so you can see what's actually involved.

For the daily declutter, you'll spend 15 minutes decluttering one assigned room. Here's the schedule that works for me. You can create a schedule that works for you based on your home layout.

Monday	kitchen
Tuesday	living room
Wednesday	bedrooms
Thursday	bathrooms
Friday	office area
Saturday	extra (garage, basement, or attic storage)
Sunday	rest

Each day, you will take 15 minutes to declutter your assigned room. If you have more than one bedroom, you will only spend 15 minutes decluttering one of the bedrooms. (Not 15 minutes on three bedrooms, totaling 45 minutes. Ain't nobody got time for that.) If you have extra rooms, like a playroom or multiple bedrooms, you'll need to rotate them each week.

For the deep declutter, pick the room that is driving you the craziest. For the next several weeks, you will spend one hour decluttering that room until you get to a week where you walk in and feel at peace in the room. (I feel like that tipping point is usually at about 60 percent decluttered. Yes, there is still clutter, but only you know it's there.)

PICKING THE FOCUS ROOM

Which room you choose as your focus room is totally up to you.

I surveyed the members of the Clutter Free Academy to see what room they would start in if their whole house felt out of control. I wondered if they would start with the room that was most out of control so they could make a huge difference in their home or with the easiest so they could have a small win quickly. But then something interesting happened. One of the members put another option into the poll—the room that visitors see first. After a day of polling, this answer became our clear winner.

I don't think it's important which room you pick, but I do think it's important to know why you are picking that room. Is it so you can stop having a sense of shame as people come through the door? Is it because you want to better function in that room? Know why you are picking that room and keep that goal in mind.

Say your living room keeps you up at night because you're so afraid someone is going to drop by and see the chaos. (Why do people just drop by? Ugh. Don't they know that we just hide upstairs until they go away? We have cell phones—call, people!) So your living room would be your focus room. Whatever that room is for you, whichever one is causing you the most stress, it's time to start dealing with it.

We cluttered people need to see big changes. We have been "all or nothing" our whole lives. "If I can't keep a room perfectly clean, I won't do anything about it at all" has been our motto since we were kids. But being clutter free is not "all or nothing." It is a process we have to live out every day for the rest of our lives.

I want to give you some big wins right up front, feeding your need for immediate results. I want you to see some big changes, and working on the room that is making you crazy is the win you need to keep you motivated and moving forward. I want you to feel like you are making big, positive changes in your life and home. And those changes happen in the rooms that are the most painful to face.

So many of us have been conditioned to think in terms of "before" and "after," like the pictures we see on TV shows, in magazines, and online (even in my group, Clutter Free Academy). And there is absolutely nothing wrong with those photos—they are inspirational and motivational all at the same time. But notice how the drawers are often closed in those photos. The outsides look great, but I'm guessing that the insides are in need of some help.

Imagine that you're desperate to cut your food budget. Do you cut out the carrots first, or do you cut out eating at Red Lobster? Starting your decluttering with the closet no one ever sees is just like cutting out carrots. Start with the big things first—and when it comes to decluttering, that means the room that's causing you the greatest stress.

*The big changes happen in the rooms
that are the most painful to face.*

THE 60 PERCENT GOAL

Once you pick your focus room, you are going to work on it until it's 60 percent clutter free. Why 60? Because you will never be 100 percent clutter free. Most of us can get to a place where we feel good walking into a room and experience peace when we're in there, while still knowing there is work to be done. (And let's be clear… That last 40 percent is the hardest to declutter.)

The 60 percent is the nonsense that invades our life every day: the clothes we don't wear, the coupons we'll never use, the mugs we got with a promotion and for some crazy reason decided that we need to put in our cupboards. The 40 percent includes the harder decisions: the photos that need to be sorted through, the artwork your kids made in second grade, the dishes your great-aunt gave you, the paperwork you might need someday.

The 40 percent? That can wait for now. Let's grab that low-hanging fruit and make our homes a more wonderful place to live. We can make them even more organized later on—after we've hit the 60 percent mark.

Once you get to 60 percent, I want you to pick another room to be your focus room and start decluttering that. Eventually, depending on how cluttered your house is, your entire house will be on the better side of decluttered. And that, my friend, is a beautiful thing.

Maybe it will take a few months, maybe a year. If things have been out of control for a very long time, it could be a couple of years. But please, please don't get discouraged! Just pick one day each week and mark off an hour on your calendar so you can do a deep declutter in your focus room. The rest of the week, just declutter for 15 minutes a day in your assigned room.

HOW TO DECLUTTER:
FOUR STEPS TO PREP

Let's talk about how your decluttering process is actually going to look each day.

Prep #1: The Three-Tote, Two-Bag System

This is a system you will be using in almost every room in your house, so I want you to gather up everything you'll need right now. Go grab…

- three tote bags
- a garbage bag
- a bag for recycling
- a timer

Mark one tote "Other Rooms," one "Put Away," and one "Give Away." Go through the area you plan to declutter and use the three totes to sort the contents.

"Other Rooms" Tote: Anything that doesn't belong in the area you're cleaning goes into the "Other Rooms" tote. This includes toys in the kitchen, dog brushes in the living room, report cards in the bathroom, or dishes in the bedroom.

"Put Away" Tote: This is the tote where you put things that belong in the area you're cleaning but need to be put away in the right place. If you're straightening up your bedroom, items that you would place in this tote might be clean clothes on the floor, shoes under your bed, or scarves hanging over a bedroom chair. Once you have your bedroom in order, you'll just put those items back where they belong.

"Give Away" Tote: Clothes your kids have outgrown? Check. DVDs your family will never watch again? Check. There is huge freedom in giving stuff away. Ask yourself, *Is this something I'm currently using or wearing? Does this make me happy when I see it? Will my family definitely use this in the next six months?* If you can answer yes to one or more of those questions, find a place for the item in your home. If not, away it goes.

I like to line this tote with a plastic bag, so when I've filled it up, I can take the plastic bag straight to the car and out of sight of small children and husbands who might want to "go through" that bag to see if I've decided to donate anything "good." (You know, like that toy that they haven't missed for five years, but suddenly, it turns out it was their favorite toy *ever*.)

And a friendly reminder: Don't donate garbage. It costs charities time and money to get rid of stuff you don't want. Don't be that person. Donate only those items that are in decent condition and are worthy of being resold.

Garbage Bag: Anything you don't want, isn't worthy of being donated, and can't be recycled goes in here.

Recycle Bag: Recycling regulations vary from city to city, so check with your local municipality or disposal service if you have any questions about what should be recycled and what shouldn't in your area.

Prep #2: Space Boxing

Pick an area or spot each day in the room you plan to clean—not the whole room. It needs to be a manageable space that will make you automatically feel like, *Oh, I can handle* that! Think small, like a drawer, your desktop, a file cabinet, a shelf, or a section of any workspace. A good place to start is the area that is bugging you the most. Just limit the area so decluttering isn't overwhelming and you can complete the task in a 15-minute segment.

Prep #3: Time Boxing

Time boxing is the process of taking a small goal and working hard on it for just a few minutes to get it accomplished. In this case, you want to declutter an area quickly so you don't get bogged down in minutia. Here are the steps you need to take:

First, set a small goal. When you declutter, your goal is not "clean the kitchen." Your goal is "clean out the utensil drawer" or "clear off this bookshelf." Space boxing by concentrating on a small area will help you stay focused and keep you from getting overwhelmed.

Second, set a timer for 15 minutes. Fifteen minutes may seem like too short an amount of time to get anything done, but trust me—you can make a difference in just a few minutes if you are setting goals and giving yourself a short time with which to work.

Third, work single-mindedly on that project until the timer goes off. The three-tote, two-bag system will help you stay focused and make decisions quickly. The beauty of time boxing is knowing that the alarm is going to go off. There is a little bit of false pressure that keeps you focused and moving forward. The adrenaline you experience when you're behind on a deadline becomes the adrenaline that now moves you forward. This is a small mind shift, but a real life changer.

Fourth, clean up whatever you have taken out. At the end of your fifteen minutes, take another five and put away everything you've sorted. Recycle or throw away the rest. Take the "Other Rooms" tote and go around the house putting away all the stuff in that tote. Then take the "Give Away" tote to where you gather stuff to donate or directly to your car to be donated the next time you run errands. Now your whole area will be clean and organized.

Prep #4: The Three Magic Questions

My closet is packed like one of those Pillsbury biscuit cans, yet magically contains nothing to wear. I think to myself, *This is it! I'm totally going to become a minimalist, have a capsule wardrobe, and never be stuck in this kind of indecision again.* So I start to dig in and declutter. I ready myself with donation bags and an attitude that says, "Get out of my way. I'm decluttering!" And away I go.

The first shirt is easy. It's my camo shirt, and I wear it any time it's clean. (For me, camo is the new floral.) No-brainer. It stays.

The next shirt…well, that one's easy to figure out for all the wrong reasons. It was a promo T-shirt an acquaintance sent me for her book launch. (I've noticed one thing about giveaway T-shirts: People order smalls, mediums, larges, and extra-larges to send out. If you are bigger than an XL, well, you still get an XL—and you're gonna like it. Friend, next time, save the postage.) Out it goes. This decluttering stuff is so easy!

Until shirt number three. It's my olive-colored tissue tee I bought at Target. I love the shirt, except it hits me in a funny place, making me wonder if my reflection in the mirror is 14 months pregnant. I can only wear the shirt with a cardigan or a zip-up sweatshirt. I do have another olive shirt that I like better, but this is a perfectly good shirt. And what if something happened to my favorite olive shirt? I would need a backup. I put it in the "maybe" pile.

Shirt number four is cute, but I don't have the right pants for it. I'm sure I will find them someday. That goes to the "maybe" pile.

In the span of forty minutes, I've got seven shirts in the "keep" pile, two in the "giveaway" pile, twenty-four in the "maybe" pile…and the rest are still hanging in the closet because it's all just too much.

The biggest problem with stuff isn't space, time, or money. It's decision fatigue. I know you want to declutter your home fast, but I also know that you will get to a point in decluttering when you are so tired of making decisions that you just…can't…do…it…anymore.

At these times, it helps to remember that we are not supposed to own a specific item for the rest of our lives. Yes, it's great when we can use and love a throw pillow for 15 years or wear that pair of pajama pants every week for a decade. But many of us love to change things up, and when we do, it's important to make way for the new by handing down the old. Because here's the thing, friend: You don't get any gold stars for having the most clothes.

And this isn't just a problem for people with a lot of extra money. I remember when I was unemployed and underemployed as a single mom. Instead of buying clothes I loved, I would buy clothes I could afford at cheap discount stores. Those clothes eventually ended up in the "maybe" pile, but I never made the decision to get rid of them. When I look back at my past attempts at decluttering, I've finally come to this conclusion: Clutter is indecision.

So how do we get over the obstacle of holding on to things that are crowding our lives? How do we regain the power to make decisions? You need to ask yourself three clear questions:

1. *Do I love it?*

2. *Do I use it?*

3. *Would I buy it again?*

As you start decluttering, write those questions down on a Post-it note. Having them in front of you while you're decluttering will help you stay focused.

If you answer no to two of those questions, I'm guessing that item is truly clutter and it's time to get rid of it. Here's how I answered those questions for two of the shirts in my "maybe" pile:

Shirt #3—The Olive Shirt

1. *Do I love it?* No. I don't want to look pregnant.

2. *Do I use it?* Occasionally, when I'm desperate.

3. *Would I buy it again?* No, it doesn't look good on me.

It's clutter. Time to go.

Shirt #4—The Shirt That Doesn't Go with Anything

1. *Do I love it?* Yes.

2. *Do I use it?* No.

3. *Would I buy it again?* No.

It's clutter. Time to go.

For me, the closet is the hardest place to make these decisions. If I can do it there, I can do it with my bookshelves and the boxes in the garage no one has opened since the day we moved in.

THERE'S ALWAYS A PRICE

In one way or another, you are paying for every single item you store.

You are paying for it in time. When you store things, it takes time to put them away, find them, and then make a decision about them every time you come across them.

You are paying for it with energy. Every item you store takes energy to move to the side while you're looking for other things.

You are paying for it with space. You can't find anything easily in a jammed storage space.

You are paying for it emotionally. Clutter affects your stress levels. Every item you remove from your home brings you one step closer to a sense of peace.

THE MIND GAME

Decluttering is all about what goes on in your head. If you tell yourself you've got this, then you can tackle the clutter a lot more easily than if you think that you're never going to get through all the piles.

Give yourself a goal. Recently, I was going through my jewelry. I hadn't gone through it in years and found a lot of things I no longer wore. I gave myself the goal of getting rid of 30 pieces of jewelry.

Because I had a goal, I got rid of some pieces that I might have been tempted to hold on to "just in case." But the best part of getting rid of the 42 (yes, 42!) pieces was that I actually rediscovered some pieces I really love and have started wearing them again. So not only do I love them (yes to question number one), but now I also use them (yes to question number two).

Think about the next owner. When I'm decluttering, I think about when I was broke and shopping at thrift stores. When I found a shirt I loved that actually fit, I was so grateful it was in my budget. If you are having a hard time parting with something you like but don't use, picture the person who will be wearing it in three weeks—how that jacket you never wear is now one of her favorite pieces of clothing. Or how that blazer made it possible for her to walk into a job interview with confidence.

The next time you are ready to declutter, arm yourself with the three magic questions, a couple of plastic bags, and a prayer of determination. You can declutter. You can make decisions. You can love your stuff again.

<><><><><><><><><><><><><>

*The more time you spend
decluttering, the more time you
earn back from cleaning.*

<><><><><><><><><><><><><>

FREQUENTLY ASKED QUESTIONS

Let's take a moment to address some of the questions you might be pondering.

What if I don't know where an item goes?

One of the questions I receive from a lot of people is, "How do I put things away if I don't know where they actually go?" For example, say you get a gift from someone, like a vase, but it doesn't have a home yet. Here is how you would evaluate that vase:

First, ask yourself, *Do I really want to keep the item?* If you can't figure out where it goes in your home, maybe there isn't a place in your home for it. I have received gifts that I couldn't use, weren't my taste, or I didn't need. I don't honor the giver any more by keeping it in my house for six months and then giving it away than I do by giving it to charity immediately. Some people may see that as cold, but let me be clear: I value the act of gift giving, even if the item I receive isn't what I needed. It gives me joy to get it into the hands of someone who could actually use it.

Second, if you do want to keep the item, at least get it into the right room. You might not be sure where to put that vase you love, but it's green, and you realize it would look great in your bedroom. At least get it into your bedroom, even if it doesn't have a spot yet. When it comes time to declutter your bedroom, the vase will be in the right place for you to reevaluate.

What if I miss a day of decluttering?

If you miss a day, I really encourage you to pick up with the next day and not try to go back and declutter the day you missed. Don't worry— the clutter isn't going anywhere! I don't want you to punish yourself because life got busy and you couldn't spend 15 minutes decluttering under your son's bed (and I won't tell if you don't). If you miss a day, wait until next week. Don't try to do it all at once.

What if I want to declutter for more than 15 minutes?

Hey friend—go with the flow! If you have some extra time, the kids are out of the house, or you're just in the groove, go for it. But if you are that excited and have an hour, how about working on your focus room for that hour? Then, during the rest of the week, do your 15 minutes per room. If you still want to do more than 15 minutes, fab!

What if I never have time to declutter?

Here is the secret that no one tells you (I don't know why; it's such life-giving information): The more time you spend decluttering, the more time you earn back from cleaning. Mind blowing, right? But I tell you, it's 100 percent true. Think about it: How much time does it take to wipe down your counter when it has piles of schoolwork, mail, and dishes that need to be done? Now, how long does it take to wipe down your counter when there is nothing on it?

Boom! Decluttering will earn you back not just days, but weeks over your lifetime. I don't know about you, but that makes me want to declutter all the livelong day.

You can declutter. You can make decisions. You can love your stuff again.

EARNING THE RIGHT TO STAY

When you're asking yourself the three questions—*Do I love it? Do I use it? Would I buy it again?*—you're really asking one big question: *Has this item earned the right to stay in this room?*

If the answer is no, you have two options: store it or get it out of the house, which means tossing it in the garbage, recycling it, or donating it.

Let's see how this works in the kitchen.

My dream kitchen is the one on *America's Test Kitchen*—my favorite cooking show ever. They have plenty of beautiful, open storage options, tons of counter space, and a clean towel every time they turn around.

Heaven.

I want you to think about how you want your kitchen to feel "stuff-wise." Are you dreaming of empty counters where you have room to actually prepare food? Are you fantasizing about cabinets that don't spill cookie sheets on you every time you open the door?

That's the dream, baby. Your kitchen is some of your most valuable real estate in your home. I want you to have a kitchen that is easy for you to work in, where you don't have to shove aside a bunch of non-sense to function in it. But let's face it—a lot of us have a lot of non-sense in our kitchens. A lot of items that haven't earned the right to stay in that room. Consider the following:

- a drawer full of paper plates from past birthdays that you've been saving for "just the right occasion"…for the last three years

- the heart-shaped cupcake pan you use every Valentine's Day to bake cupcakes for your family

- the shamrock cookie cutter you used to make Saint Patrick's Day cookies once

- the set of dishes you use only for special occasions (Of course, there has yet to be an occasion special enough to warrant bringing out those plates.)

- twelve mixing bowls (Let me repeat that: twelve mixing bowls.)

- the roasting pan you use every Thanksgiving

Let's go through these items one by one:

- *The paper plates for birthdays:* Please stop waiting to use "designer" paper plates. Use them the next time you eat away from home or have a barbecue. Otherwise, if you will never, ever use those plates again, throw them away or donate them.

- *The heart-shaped cupcake pan:* If you use it once a year, you need to keep it—but has it earned the right to be in your kitchen year-round? It can go into storage with an easy way for you to find it, or it can stay in the kitchen on a shelf that has to be accessed with a ladder.

- *The shamrock cookie cutter you used once:* Time to donate it to a family or teacher who will actually use it.

- *The special-occasion dishes:* Give yourself a challenge: *Can I use these dishes in the next year?* Put a Post-it note on them with the date. If you haven't used them in a year, it's time to say goodbye.

- *Twelve mixing bowls:* I'm sure you have four that you use over and over again. Free up the other eight for another family who will be so, so grateful to have them.

- *The roasting pan you use every Thanksgiving:* Yes, you can keep it—otherwise, your next turkey-less Thanksgiving will be super awkward. But it doesn't need to stay in your kitchen if your kitchen is crowded. It can go into storage— just make sure you can find that storage place later.

It is so easy to just collect things because we could use them at some point. But when you start to ask if those things have earned the right to stay in your valuable space, you can see what's working for you and what you're working for.

Yes, you can have 25 mugs. But if you use the same three mugs over and over again, why keep the ones you never touch? Do you have images of hot chocolate parties where you will need 25 mugs? If so, ask yourself if you've ever had a hot chocolate party, or if you are planning on one—as in, it's on the calendar. If so, feel free to keep those 25 mugs if it becomes an annual tradition. If not, it's time to shrink your collection down to just the mugs that you use, love, and would buy again.

The mental switch is that you must—absolutely must—learn to value your space. When you start to see your home for the gift it is, you long to take care of it and toss anything that doesn't serve you, your family, or your guests.

BECOMING CLUTTER FREE IS A JOURNEY

— Mandi —

When I first discovered Kathi Lipp's Clutter Free Academy, I knew I struggled with clutter but never knew how to get rid of it. I would purge in fits and starts, but I never had a system and never made a huge difference in my piles of stuff. I'd think, *What if I need those items someday? Or, I spent a lot of money on that—I can't just get rid of it!* I definitely liked to hold on to a lot of things, but I felt suffocated by all of it.

Kathi's method taught me to approach my clutter with a different perspective. I didn't need to get rid of everything in one day. By starting with one drawer or shelf and taking just a few minutes a day to declutter, I could make slow but steady progress. Instead of looking around and asking what I wanted to get rid of, I started asking what I wanted to *keep*. I'm learning to purge more and buy less.

One area where I've made the most progress is in handling paper. My husband and I had never developed a system for dealing with it. He had begun to see the transformation in other areas of the house, so when I approached him about a plan to handle and get rid of our paperwork, he was all in. He and I were able to tweak Kathi's Life Organization File (LOF) to fit our own family's needs. Within a few weeks, the piles of papers had all but disappeared. We shredded more than two big boxes' worth of papers. While we still have more paper to sort, we've gotten rid of most of it, and the LOF keeps us on track.

I can now recognize how clutter has been holding me back from moving forward. Clearing the physical clutter has given me mental clarity as well. I'm learning to be content with fewer things and in my relationship with God. By holding on to Him instead of my stuff, I'm more in tune with Him and prepared to go wherever He may call me.

Step 4

DO YOUR THING

You've dedicated your space. You've decided how you want it to feel. And you've decluttered 60 percent of that area.

So now it's time to have a little fun and play. You get to create the house you want, room by room. And here is the good news: This is a guilt-free activity! You've taken the time to really think through your house, and you've done the hard work of making your space significantly clutter free.

You? Are amazing.

So now you get to move from all the hard work of decluttering to the exciting task of really making that room yours. You get to design the house you've always wanted.

WHY I DIDN'T DECORATE (OR DO MUCH OF ANYTHING) IN THE PAST

For most of my life, I spent very little money, time, or energy decorating. It's not that I don't enjoy a well decorated room. I think there is something almost spiritual about a well-appointed space in a home. A place that promotes connection, a space that inspires, a room that contains beauty and order and peace. I just never knew how to get there.

Here were some of my issues as a cluttered person:

I never had a blank canvas. When I had so much clutter in my life, I felt like I needed to get to ground zero before I could start decorating. And I never arrived at ground zero.

I didn't feel like I deserved a nice room. This is a mind-set so many of us cluttered people deal with. "If I can't keep it nice," we ask, "why bother at all?"

I didn't have confidence in my own taste. I've never liked any of the rooms in my home, so in my brain, that meant I didn't have good taste.

Financially, decorating seemed beyond me. My money had always been in such a mess that the thought of putting aside cash for decorating seemed like a far-off dream.

Maybe some of these concerns resonate with you. So let's work through them together.

Needing a blank canvas: By working through the steps in this book— and repeating them daily—I finally have rooms with space. It's amazing how space allows me to get creative. It's actually fun to think and plan and dream about our house now that most of the clutter is gone.

Deserving a nice room: I still struggle with these feelings on a pretty regular basis. The idea I've had to come to is this: It is not selfish to want a beautiful home. In fact, it's a way that you care for yourself and others in your life. I love to have people over, and the more my home feels like me—and not the bathrobe-wearing crazy woman it can feel like when it's full of clutter—the more I'm willing to have people over at the last minute, the easier it is to invite a neighbor inside to have coffee, and the more I want to connect with people.

I've also realized that the more my house feels like the sane me, the more relaxed and at peace I am in my own home. Trust me (and everyone who loves me)—that is an investment we should all want to make. When I become healthier emotionally and spiritually, my health is reflected in my house. The converse is also true: The more clutter free and organized my home is, the more at peace I am in it.

Having confidence in your own taste: I'd never given myself the time and commitment to discover my own style. I knew the things I liked, but I didn't take time and energy to put them together. I think most of the time my prevailing thought was, *Why bother? It's just going to get cluttered anyway.* I have to tell you that this mind-set can become deeply entrenched, and that nonsense has to stop right this second.

Once you start decluttering, you are going to discover more of who you are in every area of your life. This can be exciting and overwhelming at the same time. You are going to take your home to one layer of beautiful by getting the clutter out. You will walk into a room and, instead of experiencing anxiety, there will be peace and invitation. It just happened to me this morning as I came downstairs. There was no visible clutter, the dishes were in the dishwasher (not piled up on the counters or in the sink), and I let out a little sigh of peace. When you've lived in a cluttered house all your life, you will never take entering a clutter-free room for granted.

> To grow confidence in your own taste and abilities, I suggest starting with some decorating books that don't insist on your plopping down thousands of dollars in a showroom to make your "look" come together. Instead, find some books that encourage you to use what you have and love, and slowly add in pieces as you find them and can afford them. Some of my favorite decorating books are *The DIY Home Planner* by KariAnne Wood and *The Nesting Place* and *Cozy Minimalist Home* by Myquillyn Smith.

You may be wary of getting into decorating your space, but what I've come to understand is that the more intentional we are about beautifying our rooms, the more intentional we are about keeping the nonsense out of our homes. You have earned the right to make your space your own.

Decorating without much money: Being a cluttered person in my home translated to being a cluttered person in my finances. Now that

I've had some victory in both those areas, I can save up for home furnishings and decorations I love.

Being intentional about my space *and* my money means I'm not buying "cute" stuff that just becomes clutter the same day I bring it home. Now I have a list of things I really want for my house. Maybe it's resources for a project as big as restoring the bathroom or a purchase as small as a particular vase for my living room. Either way, I buy home items on purpose, not just because they look "cute" in the moment.

*The more intentional we are
about beautifying our rooms, the more
intentional we are about keeping
the nonsense out of our homes.*

MAKE IT YOURS

If you're anything like me (and if you're reading this book, I'm guessing we have a few things in common), you've approached the whole nesting and decorating challenge with a certain amount of dread. I am missing the decorating gene. I can walk into a house and know I love it, but to achieve that look myself? Not in a million years. While I love an eclectic look, my "eclectic" can just look messy.

I'm definitely not a minimalist (let's be clear—most of us who deal with clutter just aren't), and I'm not a maximalist. I just want a room that I feel comfortable in and makes others feel welcome. That should be simple, right? But if you're missing the decorating gene, you are scared to do anything—because you've had to live with a lot of decorating mistakes in the past.

Please tell me I'm not alone in giving in to the hideous decorating trends of each decade. In the '80s I had geese flying in my kitchen. In the '90s I tried to make the space look like the Italian Riviera with faux finish on everything and wallpaper that featured a grape border. In the

2000s it was all farmhouse—but not the great, rustic farmhouse look we see today. It was more like "Old MacDonald Had a Farm," complete with red barns and too many chickens.

Yes, I've been in deep decorating denial of my past mistakes, and now I'm having flashbacks.

Let's take a deep breath. We can do this together (I say in a soft, soothing voice). You've done a ton of the decorating prep by making decisions in step 2. Remember, you have already figured out how you want your room to feel because we talked about your five senses and what will make you happy.

For me, I can start to make my kitchen my own. I'll order Mrs. Meyer's lemon verbena dish soap for the kitchen, and next month, when I have a little more money, I'll buy dish towels that I love to look at and touch. Each day, as I continue to declutter and make decisions about the room, the space will become a little more *me*.

BUYING WHAT YOU LOVE

CH (Cluttered Home) people want to buy their way to good feelings. (I don't say that as a judgment. I say it with a ton of personal history.) We feel unfulfilled in some part of our lives, so we go and buy the cute cat scrub brush holder (or whatever your equivalent is). But no matter how cute it was on the store shelf, when we get it home among all the clutter, it just becomes one more distraction from what's really going on emotionally. (This is the whole reason that Target has a dollar section. We feel like we can't afford to spend $300 on a piece of furniture we love, but we will spend a dollar 300 times because something is cute.)

So what do you do when you are at that flea market and you find the perfect item…but you didn't know that you needed it until you saw it?

First, ask yourself where it's going to live in your house. It's not enough to say, "I love it!" You have to be able to say, "I love it, and I know exactly where it's going. And I know what I'm going to give away in order to make room for it." Second, remember that you're buying for now *and* for the future. Don't buy anything that makes you say, "I know I'll want this for later." Buy what you will use now and for years to come.

Get the candle. Or the picture frame, or the table, or the vase. But don't get it because it's on sale. Get it because it's the exact one you were dreaming of.

<hr>

When you've lived in a
cluttered house all your life,
you will never take entering a
clutter-free room for granted.

<hr>

CURATION

Recently, my stepson, Jeremy, went to a concert for a band he has loved since high school. While he was at the concert, he ran into my daughter's boyfriend, Mahan. Mahan was there with a friend who had VIP passes and got to have a "backstage experience" with the band. He got a signed poster out of the deal.

Mahan wasn't actually a big fan of the band—he was there just to be with his friend. When he ran into Jeremy and found out how much he loved this band, Mahan gave him the signed poster. Jeremy was thrilled, and the very next day he went to Michaels to have the poster framed.

Jeremey has been to dozens of concerts in his life, but he only kept the poster for this particular band. And not only did he keep the poster, but instead of stuffing it in a corner or under a chair, he had it framed so that he could enjoy it for years to come.

That, my friend, is curation.

Curation is the act of winnowing down your stuff, keeping the best of it, and making it shine. It is surrounding yourself with beautiful, meaningful things that make you happy. Pick the best, make it part of your room, and get rid of the rest.

THE 11 R'S OF DECORATING ON A BUDGET

Keep these tips in mind as you do your thing in each room.

1. Remove

If you're a clutter girl, my guess is that you still need to remove some things from your room (even if you've decluttered 60 percent of the space). What in that room do you not use or love? What wouldn't you choose to buy again? Out those things go. Still feeling chaotic? Remove even more until that room feels at rest. I would rather you have 10 items that sparkle and tell your story than 30 that you like but get lost in the chaos.

If you're scared to take an item out, remove it for a day and see how you feel when you walk into the room. When something's missing, you can either miss the item or feel relieved at the change. See how removing the object makes you feel and go with that feeling.

2. Re-home

When you are removing items from one room, carefully consider whether they would make sense (and would make you so very happy) in another room. I've moved throw pillows from my living room into our master bedroom, moved a set of aqua vases from our kitchen to our living room, and am forever trying quilts that my mom has made in one room or another. Sometimes I need to sit with an item for a while before I decide where it's going to live forever (or more likely, for now).

3. Rediscover

Using what you already have is one of the most beautiful things about getting clutter free. In all that clutter you bought (or collected, or inherited from relatives who are trying to declutter), you have some good stuff, but you may have forgotten about it. Maybe it was packed away in storage, or maybe it was buried. Now that you're living lighter, you can see what you already own.

4. Repurpose

Sometimes I use quilts as wall hangings, glasses as vases, books as levels to display art, a ladder as shelving, or a tray as a side table. If your brain doesn't think like that, you can always go on Pinterest to get ideas for repurposing the things you love. But don't hold on to things with the hope of repurposing them "someday." It's better to get rid of them now and make room for the items you will actually use. Let someone who is good at figuring out "funky" find your treasure and do something with it.

5. Renovate

I had a red IKEA hutch in our kitchen for years that I just loved, but it wasn't very useful because it was pretty much a bookshelf with a cabinet. So Roger took a saw to it and created holes so that I could string the cords to my coffee maker through it, created new holes for the shelves so I could accommodate the height of my coffee maker and canisters, and installed hooks so I could hang lighting from the top.

6. Revamp

Maybe the item needs to be revamped to make it what you need it to be. One of my favorite projects that I've done involved taking a vintage map that was in a box in the garage and putting it in a frame to hang on our wall. In the past, I've also put postcards in frames and had a friend sew pom-poms onto a pillow.

7. Refresh

I love to decorate using the nature around me. We have a couple of rose bushes in the front yard that I only recently started cutting to bring the blooms indoors. I also have access to some olive branches that look beautiful in a vase. Take a fresh look at your front yard and backyard to see what you can use to spruce up your space in a clutter-free way.

8. Rearrange

Oftentimes, when I bring something home, I think of it as a stand-alone item. (*That picture would look cute on my office wall.*) But most of the time, if I really love something and want to make it work, it ends up in a grouping. So instead of having one picture on an office wall, I have a grouping of items that all belong together.

For example, I have a hand lettered canvas with the word *Love* written over and over again, a letter *K* that a friend painted for me, a big aqua clock, a sign with an inspirational quote, and a stained book that my son gave me with the pages folded over in a specific way to spell out the word *Woof* (combining my love of dogs and reading). All of these things on their own in my office would look like clutter, but because I've grouped them together, they form a cute, personal vignette that describes who I am.

9. Restore

I think that plain old cleaning is highly underrated as a decorating strategy. Sweeping the floor, polishing the wood, and scrubbing toilets are all ways of making your house seem way more "together."

10. Rethink

Once you declutter, you have the physical (not to mention the mental) space to do some projects that you've been longing to do. My mom handed down a huge living room coffee table to our kids Amanda and Shaun. It was a little too big for their tiny apartment, so we swapped our smaller table with theirs and took my mom's old table. Roger sanded it, and I painted it an orange red (it's cuter than it sounds). It looks amazing in our living room by our giant wraparound couch.

This was only possible because three generations (my mom, ourselves, and our kids) were all willing to rethink our space. Everyone was happy with what they got (or got rid of).

Be willing to rethink what you need to make your space work—and then work with other people. If you have the perfect yellow pillow that would look great at your sister's house, be willing to think outside the four walls of your own home.

11. Release

I've been known to say to friends and family, "If you're ever looking to get rid of that chair [or those vases, etc.], let me know. I'd love to consider buying it." You never know when someone might get tired of their stuff. Always be more than fair—be generous in these situations. You want the memories and feelings associated with the objects in your house to be good ones.

I do this in the opposite direction as well. If someone consistently tells me how much they love something in my home, I make a mental note for the day when I'm ready to release that item. Maybe they want it for their home, or maybe they loved the item in my home, but it's not for them. Either way, I'm always thinking of my stuff as alive and moving (and not dead and buried in the garage.)

When we discover the clutter-free way of life, we are released from the fear of having to hold on to stuff forever. Remember, we do not hold on to things for "someday." We release things that no longer serve who we are or who we want to be.

— PART 2 —

THE SPACES

THE KITCHEN

have had every kind of kitchen known to man.

I remember as a little girl walking through the house my parents would eventually buy and hearing the real estate agent proudly calling the kitchen a "cake kitchen"—that is, you can easily reach everything you would ever need in order to bake a cake while standing in one place. I'm pretty sure he made up that term (have you ever heard of a "cake kitchen" before?) in order to sell my parents Barbie's dream kitchen.

My first kitchen as an adult was in a tiny apartment where I was a missionary in Uji, Japan. My fridge was of the "what college kids use to store their ramen" size and had room to store five plates, five bowls, and five cups. (The number four is considered bad luck in Japan. It took me all year to wrap my head around having five of everything.)

Yes, I did get a bigger kitchen when I moved back to the States, but most of my kitchens have been of the "appropriate for an Easy Bake Oven" size. And with the size of our family, I learned that in order to work in a small space, I needed to hold function over form. In other words, it didn't matter what the kitchen looked like, I just needed to be able to get food on the table before the townspeople decided to organize and rise up.

While I want most of my house to be warm, cozy, and inviting, I really want a different feel for my kitchen. Of all the rooms, this is where I want to get stuff done more than look at pretty décor. My main objective in the kitchen is to make sure I have the space and tools I need to get meals prepped and on the table.

Your objective may be different than mine—and in your kitchen, you get to decide. Let's get you started, using the four steps we've already gone through: dedicate, decide, declutter, and do your thing.

DEDICATE

As you dedicate your kitchen, remember, you're naming the top five intended uses for this space. In my home, those uses are cooking, eating, connecting, working, and storing food. Write down the uses of your own space at the end of this chapter.

Maybe, like me, you're finding that your kitchen is a multipurpose room used for a variety of tasks. But as you start to declutter, keep these purposes in mind. If you come across something in the kitchen that doesn't fit one of the five purposes you wrote about, it's time to either move the item to the appropriate room or give it away.

I shared earlier about the sign in our kitchen that declares, "The Lipp-Smackin' Café—Sit Long, Talk Much." Here are some other wording ideas for signs you could put up in the kitchen:

- "Meals and memories are made here."

- "Cooking with love provides food for the soul."

- "People who love to eat are always the best people" (Julia Child).[4]

- "Jesus declared, 'I am the bread of life. Whoever comes to me will never go hungry, and whoever believes in me will never be thirsty'" (John 6:35).

- "Taste and see that the LORD is good; blessed is the one who takes refuge in him" (Psalm 34:8).

DECIDE

Now it's time to ask how you want your kitchen to *feel*. This space is just for dreaming—we'll put all of this into action after decluttering. But I want to give you a vision for why you're going to bother decluttering and what your kitchen will feel like when you get there. The rewards will be amazing.

As a reminder, I want my own kitchen to feel clean, comfortable, creative, cozy, and connectional. Here's how I'm working on creating those feelings:

Sight: When I walk into the kitchen, I want to see clean counters, place mats on the table, and a sign for our family. I need great lighting, and I need to do the dishes every night.

Smell: In my kitchen, I love the smells of my favorite dish soap, candles, and coffee brewing in the morning.

Taste: I want to taste that coffee too! I also love to have a selection of teas available for our guests, and I want to be able to access our meal plan at a glance.

Touch: I want nice dish towels so I don't dread doing those dishes.

Sound: I need a quiet dishwasher so I can hear my audiobook through the speakers.

At the end of this chapter, you'll find space to describe how you want your own kitchen to feel.

Zones

As you make decisions about your kitchen, be honest with yourself about how you use it. If you don't enjoy cooking and end up using DoorDash more often than not, you can afford to have a kitchen that is more cute than functional. But if you are a chef at heart, you'll need to spend extra time thinking through the organization of the kitchen.

One of the quickest ways to bring a sense of order to the kitchen is to create zones. If you love to bake, create a baking station where you always have all your ingredients together, right alongside your favorite mixing bowls, measuring cups and spoons, stand mixer, and rolling pin.

I have a shelf in my kitchen that is dedicated to all things Instant Pot. I love that everything I need is in one area, and I can pull together a meal in minutes. Of course, I also have a coffee zone. I have big glass containers with ground and whole coffee beans and filters. I have two coffee makers (a Keurig, and a coffee maker for everyday drinks), plus an array of flavorings, containers for sugar and sweeteners, coffee cups, and more. (Did I mention that we take our coffee very seriously around here?)

Divide your own kitchen into zones using the page at the end of this chapter.

DECLUTTER

Repeat after me: "I will not try to declutter the kitchen all in one day."

Please. Say it one more time. "I will not try to declutter the kitchen all in one day."

The kitchen can be an overwhelming place to declutter. That is why it is so important that you take it one shelf, one drawer, one counter at a time.

Here is a list of all the areas and categories in your kitchen that might need to be decluttered. If you don't have an area that is listed here—congrats! You get a check mark without even decluttering. If you have extra areas to declutter, put them on the list and thank God for His abundance in your life.

- ☐ silverware
- ☐ other utensils
- ☐ dishes
- ☐ glassware
- ☐ mugs
- ☐ pots and pans
- ☐ pantry (each individual shelf)

- ☐ coffee area
- ☐ small appliance storage
- ☐ serving dishes
- ☐ wrap drawer (plastic wrap, aluminum foil, bags)
- ☐ storage containers (Note: Toss any containers or lids that don't match.)
- ☐ The Mysterious and Little-Visited Region Under the Sink
- ☐ refrigerator
- ☐ freezer
- ☐ bar cart
- ☐ microwave cart
- ☐ kitchen towels
- ☐ pot holders
- ☐ aprons
- ☐ place mats
- ☐ cloth napkins
- ☐ kitchen island
- ☐ medicines
- ☐ tiny cabinet over the fridge that no one can reach
- ☐ water bottles
- ☐ paper and plastic cups, plates, and silverware
- ☐ cookbooks
- ☐ coupons
- ☐ spices
- ☐ baking supplies
- ☐ counters (if they are really cluttered, take them in sections)

☐ rarely used items (turkey platter, holiday dishes, etc.)

☐ any other kitchen furniture you may have

☐ space above the cupboards

☐ miscellaneous (vases, candleholders, etc.)

When you set your timer to declutter, pick one area or category of items. If you finish it up before the timer goes off, feel free to move to the next area. Keep decluttering until you feel like your room is mostly decluttered. Don't worry—even though the decluttering will continue, once you've got the room mostly decluttered, it's time to do some of the fun stuff.

DO YOUR THING

You've worked hard, made decisions (that's the hardest part of all this, isn't it?), and decluttered. And now that you've spent time loving your kitchen back into a place where you can function, it's time to put your family's personality into your space. Even if you're like me and want your kitchen to be, above all, functional, that doesn't mean you can't put a little "fun" in the functional.

Since my kitchen is tiny and is all cabinets and tile, the only space I really have to work with is the kitchen window and one wall. Here are a few low-cost things I've done to infuse some personality into my workspace:

- I replaced the white knobs on my white cabinets with brushed nickel knobs. It's a small change, but it makes the kitchen look so much more pulled together with our stain-less-steel appliances.

- I bought new (cheap) window shades at Home Depot (you can buy them and have them cut in store—mine cost a total of $75). I've used this kind of shade before, and it looks great.

- I ordered my Mrs. Meyer's lemon verbena dish soap, hand

soap, and lotion. It makes me happy every single time I smell it. (I look like one of those crazy women sniffing her dish soap on TV commercials.)

- I set up a playlist on Amazon (we have an Echo in the kitchen) with different types of music. (Rend Collective is my current favorite.)

- My kitchen counters are dark green—not my current favorite color. But when I priced out the cost of having new counters installed… Let's just say that I'm learning to love the dark green ones. Now I'm on the hunt for some artwork and accessories that will combine what I want (white and turquoise) with what I have (dark green).

- A not-so-cheap fix: lighting. But since ours was original to the house and installed by someone who thought that wiring laws were "suggestions" and liked to get creative, it was time to rip out the "ode to the '70s" fluorescent lights. The new lights make my whole kitchen seem lighter and brighter, and I love working in this space all over again.

Of course, I still have a "someday" list. (I'd love a new glass door and a kitchen island!) This home will always be a work in progress—and so will yours.

For most of us, the kitchen is the hub of our family's activities. Gathering around the table brings us together in ways other activities can't. An inviting atmosphere draws our people in and serves to nourish our family's emotional needs as well as their physical needs. A clean kitchen can help you provide wholesome, healthy food, but making it a warm, inviting space will also provide food for the soul.

MAKE YOUR KITCHEN WORK FOR YOU

1. Clear out the cupboards so you can get to your baking dishes and bowls easily.

2. Clear off the kitchen table so you and your family can eat dinner and work as needed.

3. Dedicate a cabinet to company and fill it with place mats, dishes, cups, and silverware.

4. Clean out the pantry and check the expiration dates on all the food you're storing.

5. Set up dedicated zones for your family's needs.

MY TOP FIVE

THE TOP FIVE USES
OF MY KITCHEN

1. _____

2. _____

3. _____

4. _____

5. _____

THE FIVE WAYS I WANT
MY KITCHEN TO FEEL

1. _____

2. _____

3. _____

4. _____

5. _____

MY KITCHEN THROUGH
MY FIVE SENSES

Sight: _____

_____

_____

Smell: _____

_____

_____

Taste: _____

_____

_____

Touch: _____

_____

_____

Sound: _____

_____

_____

MY KITCHEN'S ZONES

THE LIVING ROOM

've never had—and as far as I can see, never *will* have—a formal living room. And I am perfectly fine with that life choice. Our living room has always been of the "multipurpose" nature. It has never been the kind of room that we keep nice for company coming over—it always has too much life running through it.

While the kids were young, the living room was the main play area. When the kids were older, we kept the computer monitors in that highly visible area so we could keep an eye on the kids' online activities. As you can guess, that living room would not have met Joanna Gaines's standards.

And now? That living room is the space for our TV, my writing, our morning quiet time, and our projects. (I have an office for work, but my best writing is done on the couch under a quilt with a puggle sitting next to me.) And since it is the first room people see when they enter our home, my goal is to keep it as clutter free as possible. Not just for the sake of our guests, but for our own peace of mind.

DEDICATE

In my home, the top five uses of my living room are working, watching TV, connecting, reading, and snuggling. Write down the uses of your own space at the end of this chapter.

Now that I know what this room is for, I can also be clear about what it's *not* for. It's not a fussy room for "entertaining." (Such a loaded word, as if it's our job to impress people.) Actually, that's why you see me using the word *connecting* throughout this book. When I replace the word *entertaining* with *connecting*, all the pressure and dramatic air gets left out, and life becomes much simpler.

So, for me, this is a room that is about connecting and relaxing. Now that I know that, I can move the valuable antique lamp into our bedroom and replace it with an IKEA lamp. I can enjoy the antique myself instead of reserving it to impress my guests. And I won't weep over the IKEA lamp if it gets knocked over by a guest.

DECIDE

It's time to get super intentional and really think about your living room. I want my living room to feel welcoming (since it's the first room people see), cozy, soft, interesting, and warm. Here's how I'm working on creating those feelings:

Sight: There is minimal clutter. The room looks clean and inviting. The floors are cleared and picked up. I've repainted our old, hand-me-down coffee table to a dark, burnt orange and put some hand-painted drawer pulls on it to make it look custom. It went from being my least favorite piece of furniture in the room to my favorite.

Smell: My biggest goal in the living room is for it to not smell like anything (especially my dog, Jake). That is why I make Jake sit on a blanket when he is cuddling with me on the couch, and I wash those blankets regularly. In the colder months, I love to have pine or apple candles burning. In the warmer months, I like something a little more herbal, like mint or rosemary. I'm also in the process of switching from carpet to laminate floors (my wisest decision with two animals living in the house), but while I had carpet, it was important to be on a schedule for getting those carpets cleaned so they didn't trap smells.

Taste: This is where I drink my morning coffee every day. One of the best (and most useful) gifts I've ever received was a round tray that I can use on the couch to hold my coffee in the morning and iced tea in the afternoon. I've spilled one too many coffee cups to ever believe I'm coordinated enough to balance my mug.

Touch: I have loads of comfy pillows on our couch, homemade quilts from my mom, and throw blankets to cozy up with.

Sound: We have Pandora on our TV in this room, which is always playing if we are cleaning, reading, or putting together a puzzle.

Now it's your turn. At the end of the chapter, write down the five words you want to describe your living room.

Zones

What activities go on in your living room? As you really think this through, it becomes easier to create zones and make the room what it needs to be (and not some outdated version of what you think a living room should be). Here's what we decided on for our house:

The writing zone. Because I do so much writing in the living room, easy power access and lighting are important to me in the corner where I sit and work. I also have a great tray that can sit next to me on the couch (it's an *L*-shaped couch) so my coffee or water is always within reach.

The relaxing zone. My husband has his zone as well (and yes, it includes a recliner). He has a place to watch TV, work on his laptop, have a drink, and stash his snacks.

The project zone. I have an open storage table in the living room that is my "project zone." I keep projects that I'm working on in fabric file boxes so they look cute while staying contained and organized.

Think through what zones you need in your living room and be super honest with yourself. What items in this space have you just been living with instead of dealing with? What can you do to make this room more functional?

For years I had a magazine rack in our living room...because isn't that where you're supposed to read magazines? Isn't there a law of some sort that says that every American house has to have a stack of magazines in the living room? But where do I really read magazines? On the road.

Now I love to grab a magazine, flip through it, and then leave it for the next traveler or person waiting at the doctor's office. It's my clutter-free way of enjoying magazines, and it makes me super happy. Instead of having a "magazine zone" in the living room, I now have a blank space. And it's lovely.

*What have you just
been living with instead
of dealing with?*

DECLUTTER

If your living room is anything like mine, it's hard to know what to declutter because the room is used for so many different activities. That is why it is so important to take it one area at a time. Here are the basic areas of a living room that are common to many homes:

- ☐ couch area
- ☐ coffee table
- ☐ TV and entertainment center
- ☐ storage
- ☐ bookshelf
- ☐ magazine rack
- ☐ side table
- ☐ fireplace and mantel
- ☐ piano (this came up multiple times in our Clutter Free Academy group)

Remember, get to your 60-percent decluttering goal before you move on to the fun stuff. The next step will be your reward.

DO YOUR THING

Now it's time to put some *you* back in your room! All those things that you've dreamed of and imagined for your room? It's time to make them slowly come true.

If you are looking to make your living room everything you want it to be, but your budget is a little *less* than all you want it to be, it may be time to "shop" your home. This is the act of taking items in your home that you already love and finding a new way to display them—and in no room is this easier to do than in the living room. Here are just some of the items I've "re-homed" and given new life to in my living room:

- A bunch of fat ceramic chickens that used to live in my kitchen are now nesting on a bookshelf in the living room.

- I have two glass birdcages in the living room that now house turquoise, gold, and silver Christmas balls with some twinkle lights scattered throughout. I intended to have them out only for Christmas, but I loved the look so much that I've kept them up all year long.

- I took a long wooden serving tray from my kitchen and now use it in the living room to store coasters and serve coffee to guests.

- I use jelly jars to hold clippings from my garden.

- I have a pitcher and basin from our kitchen sitting on an antique washstand at the entrance to our living room.

- I've hung a large silver serving platter over the antique washstand.

- I took a turquoise and white pillow that I bought for my office and decided it looked much more at home on our living room couch.

Just because you bought something for your bedroom or kitchen doesn't mean it needs to stay in your bedroom or kitchen. It may have just been making a pit stop on the way to its real, forever home.

Most of us do a lot of "living" in our living rooms. It's the place where we declare we're done with a full day's work by plopping down on the couch with the remote or snuggling up with a good book. When your children grow up and leave the home, they will remember this room with fondness (second only to the kitchen, especially if you had hungry teenage boys). Your time and effort to declutter and make this room your own will be a gift to your family that lasts a lifetime.

MAKE YOUR LIVING ROOM
WORK FOR YOU

1. Clear out a drawer for your quiet time supplies.

2. Figure out quality lighting solutions for your space.

3. Get a snuggly blanket to create a calming atmosphere.

4. Get a basket for the remotes so they aren't randomly scattered all over the room.

5. Install blinds or heavy curtains to block out the sun on hot days and sheer drapes to allow maximum sunlight in the winter.

MY TOP FIVE

THE TOP FIVE USES
OF MY LIVING ROOM

1. _____

2. _____

3. _____

4. _____

5. _____

THE FIVE WAYS I WANT
MY LIVING ROOM TO FEEL

1. _____

2. _____

3. _____

4. _____

5. _____

MY LIVING ROOM
THROUGH MY FIVE SENSES

Sight: _____

_____

_____

Smell: _____

_____

_____

Taste: _____

_____

_____

Touch: _____

_____

_____

Sound: _____

_____

_____

MY LIVING ROOM'S ZONES

THE BEDROOM

Have you ever had one of those days?

I was grumbling and complaining because the list of household stuff that I need to get done was huge. There is nothing I hate more than stripping sheets and remaking the bed, and the *whole* thing needed to be done. Down to the dust ruffle. (I really ought to balance my need for dozens of pillows with the fact that I hate making the bed.)

So there I was, whining, when God started giving me mental pictures of the ministry that happens in this place. It's where He provides rest for me more nights than not. It's where I fall asleep on the shoulder of the man He has given me to demonstrate His love in a tangible way. It's where I've loved my kids, read His Word, and recovered when I was sick.

Because of those pictures, I chose to take the time to *dress* the bed. Hanging the comforter to dry in the sun so it smells like only sun-dried cloth can. Fluffing the pillows, spraying the linens (and let's be clear, by "linens" I'm talking HomeGoods specials—nothing too fancy), folding the quilts, and making it as comfy as possible for me and my husband.

I ended up grateful to God for providing so richly and valuing rest and connection so deeply.

Has your bedroom become the place where everything goes to die? Kids' homework, laundry piles, and unfinished projects all get shoved there because, well, nobody sees that room.

Except you. And potentially the person you love most in the world. That's all.

I know that I've felt the same way. My master bedroom was the *Friends* rerun playing while I was doing other things. It was there, but nobody was paying attention. I want your bedroom to go from an afterthought to the main event. I want your bedroom to be the place of sanctuary and rest that you've hoped it could be, but never dreamed it would be.

*I want your bedroom
to go from an afterthought
to the main event.*

DEDICATE

I would love to say that my bedroom is a sanctuary where soft music plays and my husband and I talk long into the night about life and love. That is so not my reality. What really happens in our bedroom (don't worry—I won't overshare) is this:

I wake up in the morning between 5:00 and 5:30 and sneak downstairs without turning on any lights so I don't wake up my husband. Later on that morning, I get dressed in my room. At some point during the day, I will fold laundry on top of the bed. At around 7:00 p.m., my puggle, Jake, will start getting irritated if I'm not in the bedroom, ready to snuggle. I get ready for bed, crawl under the covers, and snuggle with Jake while watching TV or reading. A little bit later, Roger will crawl into bed, we'll snuggle, and then I'll pass out.

Not super glamorous, but that's the reality of our bedroom. In looking at that list, here are the top five things my bedroom is used for:

1. rest

2. relationship (Roger and I do a lot of our dreaming and talking in bed. Plus, we are snugglers.)

3. getting ready (Our closet and dressers are in this room so we can get dressed and ready for the day.)

4. relaxing (We both like to read and watch TV in our room.)

5. restoration (Roger is a napper on the weekends, and when I'm sick, there is no place I'd rather be than in my own bed.)

Like I said—not glamorous, but real life. And that is what we are going for here: real life. Not some Pinterest or Bravo TV version of what you think your bedroom should be. (Most of us don't need an entire section of our room dedicated to a dressing table or a closet the size of a basketball court.)

Now it's your turn. I want you to spend a few minutes really thinking through what your bedroom is used for. Go ahead and list those uses at the end of the chapter so you know what your room is dedicated to and how to move forward.

If you are married, this list can be a great way to focus and dedicate this space to your relationship. Come up with words that will inspire ideas, thoughts, and prayers for who you are as a couple.

And if you are single? It may be even more important to dedicate the space for growing into who you want to be. When I was a single mom, my bedroom needed to support the person I was becoming, not a relationship. I was super broke, so I didn't have any extra money to spend on decorating my bedroom. (Any extra money needed to go to work clothes or things my kids needed.) So instead of buying artwork, I would put up Post-its with some of my favorite Bible verses and quotations. When I had a little extra money, I would buy frames at the thrift store and ask a coworker who had pretty handwriting to write those same quotations on white paper. I then put those framed pages up in my room.

Do what you can with what you have. It doesn't have to look perfect to others, just meaningful to you.

DECIDE

In my bedroom, I've decided a few things are important:

It needs to be clutter free. I sneak out each morning in the dark. Whether or not I have clutter on the floor could mean the difference between whether I trip and break my neck or not. Plus, clutter in the bedroom? Not exactly restful.

I need my clothes to be organized and ready to go. When I was living in a cluttered house, I spent way too many hours digging through laundry baskets in order to get dressed.

I need my bed to be made. I do laundry on my bed several times a week. (It's a large, flat surface, perfect for folding and piling.) A made bed makes that task so much easier. Plus, I just love the feeling of slipping into the sheets of a made bed. Love it. Making my bed is one of the little things I can do every day to take care of my future self.

I want this room to feel cozy, efficient, restful, clean, and warm. Here's how I work to create those feelings:

Sight: There is minimal clutter. The room looks clean and inviting. The floors are cleared and picked up. It's dark and cozy when I need it to be, and bright and light during the day.

Smell: I want this room to smell like fresh air and clean laundry. Sadly, this is the room where our dog spends 90 percent of his time (his choice—I promise we are not locking him up in there). We open the windows in the early mornings and evenings and make sure that we vacuum three to four times per week to keep it smelling fresh.

Taste: Not a lot of taste going on in the bedroom. I'm okay with that. That way, there are no crumbs or spills on the floor—or on my clean laundry.

Touch: I want a comfy but firm mattress that we can sink into each night. I want fluffy bedding and lots of throw pillows to relax in during the day when I'm reading a book or resting my eyes.

Sound: I want the option to enjoy TV or music—or an audiobook while I'm folding clothes.

Now it's your turn. What five feelings would you like to experience when you walk into your bedroom? List them at the end of the chapter. Then brainstorm ways you can experience those feelings through sight, smell, taste, touch, and sound. What would you like to change in your bedroom so that it creates the feeling you want to fall asleep to at night? Write down those ideas in the space at the end of the chapter.

Zones

Think through the different zones in your bedroom and how you can best organize your life to make everything that happens there easier to maintain.

The sleep zone. This is the area of your bed and nightstands, which should include everything you need to have a great night's sleep. Since Roger and I share sleeping space with a puggle and a cat, we enjoy a king-sized bed.

The clothes zone. Hopefully this isn't your bedroom floor or the chair in the corner of your room. Think about your dresser and closet and how those can be used most effectively. I adjust my storage methods according to where I'm living.

The entertainment zone. Our dog is 15 years old and starts to whine and fuss if we are not in bed at 8:30. We may be getting older, but I'm still too young for our night to be capped off before 9:00 p.m. So Roger and I crawl into bed and watch something on Netflix for 30 minutes before falling asleep. This is also the area where we keep our Alexa device and store some movies that we have on DVD.

DECLUTTER

This past week, we moved everything out of our bedroom in order to start on a remodeling project.

Have mercy.

I thought I had done a pretty good job of keeping our bedroom decluttered (and trust me, it is an order of magnitude better than it was even five years ago), but the amount of clutter that can accumulate in that room is shocking. It's easy to be "clutter blind" until you do something crazy like move. Or remodel. And we won't even discuss the amount of dog hair that was trapped between the bed and the wall. I could have fashioned a litter of puggle puppies just from that stash.

So let me say that I think you are doing hero's work by decluttering your bedroom. It is so easy to neglect this space since you're "the only one who is going to see it." It is so much more motivating to be able to clean up the living room before people come over or the kitchen so that it's easier to cook dinner in there. But the bedroom? To me, that room is filled with so many decisions that are hard to make. So let me say it loud and clear: I'm proud of you!

Following are some areas you may have to declutter—but remember not to take on too much.

- ☐ under the bed (and any storage containers there)
- ☐ armoire
- ☐ dresser
- ☐ closet
- ☐ nightstands
- ☐ desk
- ☐ window seats
- ☐ chests
- ☐ bench at the end of the bed
- ☐ chair
- ☐ top of wardrobe (storage space)
- ☐ shelves for books and knickknacks
- ☐ magazine rack
- ☐ lampstand
- ☐ media cabinets
- ☐ jewelry case
- ☐ space behind the dresser
- ☐ space between the bed and wall

DO YOUR THING

I'm guessing your bedroom has been neglected for years. We cluttered people tend to live with what we have in the parts of the house that are just for us. But now it's time to reclaim that space. Your reward for dedicating your space, deciding how it's used, and then decluttering, is getting to do your thing. You can finally have the bedroom you want—and, as someone who is working hard to take care of her home, the bedroom you deserve.

I know that you are not going to be able to make over your room in a night (this is *The Clutter-Free Home*, not the show *Trading Spaces*), but I do want you to have a plan. A plan you can look forward to and execute a little at a time.

In order to do that, I don't want you to start aimlessly wandering the aisles of Target or T.J. Maxx, picking up bright and shiny items, bringing them home, and making them try to fit into your bedroom (that may have been part of what got you into trouble in the first place). I want you to develop your plan. Think through what is going to make this room the room that you've always wanted to fall asleep in. The room that makes you eager to greet the morning.

Whether you share your room with your husband or have a space all to yourself, you want to make it as much "you" as possible. Work through the following questions to create the space you love.

What colors do you want to feature in this room?

When Roger and I got married, he let me pick the colors for every room in our house. He was happy with all my choices for the rooms except for one: our bedroom. I went with a light lavender, and he has felt *blah* about it ever since.

I picked lavender because it's light and soothing, and I thought it would help us sleep better. Roger said, "Why would the wall color help us sleep better? The lights are out. I can't see the wall color." So this time we are going bold: cream and navy with Kelly green accents. No "light and soothing" for us.

What colors would make you happy when you walk into your bedroom? Maybe you've had the same paint color for decades because your room has always been so cluttered, it just seemed like too big of a hassle to repaint it. But now that you are creating a clutter-free home, you can start thinking about how you truly want to live.

If you share this room with your spouse and they care about the color choices, it's time to compromise (in the best way possible) about the colors and style of the room. The navy blue—that's for Roger. The Kelly green? That's all me, baby. (And even though Kelly green would not be Roger's first choice in that room, I have spent sufficient time convincing him that having a bedroom I want to spend time in benefits him as well as me.)

What type of bedspread is the best fit for you?

Roger and I have been through a number of different bedspreads, comforters, and all sorts of combinations until we finally figured out what works for us: duvets.

We have a dog who is a co-sleeper. In other words, Jake the puggle is spoiled and sleeps at the foot of our bed. Most of the time. Until he gets scared and sleeps on top of my head. Fortunately for you, this is not a dog training book. We finally gave up on having comforters and bedspreads that had to be washed at the laundromat or taken to a dry cleaner. Now we use a combination of a duvet and a light bedspread for most of the year, except in the winter, when we throw a heavier electric blanket in that duvet. Now, instead of dragging everything to a dry cleaner, I just throw the duvet in the wash every few weeks and it comes out perfect.

We also have decided that we are a cream-colored duvet family. (See Jake the puggle above. Cream puggle hair does not show up on a cream duvet. Just saying…) Think through what is going to look great but also be easy to clean and take care of based on how you really live—not how you *feel* you should live or how your mother-in-law lives.

What type of sheets do you want?

Again, this is something that should be thought through carefully. I love a good set of flannel sheets in the winter, but Roger can't stand them. So we've compromised on some brushed cotton sheets. They don't get too hot for Roger, and I don't feel like I'm slipping and sliding, which makes me happy.

What kind of mattress is best for you?

We bought traditional mattresses for years and thought, *We must be tougher on mattresses than any other two human beings on the planet.* After about three years, we hated how saggy and lumpy our expensive mattresses were.

And then we ordered a Tuft and Needle.

I doubt that Roger and I will ever buy any other mattress again. (And no, I don't get a commission from them.) For some people they are just too firm, but we find them the perfect combo of firm and snuggly.

We've actually had friends ask to try out our mattress to see if it would be the right firmness for them. Another friend ordered a Tuft and Needle mattress, and after about a month of sleeping on it, she decided it was not what they wanted. Tuft and Needle let her donate it to a charitable organization and gave her a full refund. That's the kind of company I want to support.

The most important thing when it comes to your bedroom is not to let it come together on accident. Think of your room as the first priority, not the place of last resort. We give our best when we work from a place of rest, and our bedrooms provide a sanctuary from all the busyness of life.

Even if no one else sees your bedroom (remember how I said I don't offer tours of my house?), you deserve to have an uncluttered, peaceful space you love. I want you to have a place to recharge so you can be free to live out the life for which God created you.

1. Declutter your clothes and clean out your closet.

2. Clean out the drawer of your nightstand so you have room for vitamins, chargers, or any other personal items you need.

3. Have a bed that is easy to make.

4. Be reasonable about the number of pillows you pile on the bed because you'll have to remove them each night and replace them in the morning.

5. If you have a small bedroom, use lighter colors to create a feeling of more space.

MY TOP FIVE

THE TOP FIVE USES
OF MY BEDROOM

1. _____

2. _____

3. _____

4. _____

5. _____

THE FIVE WAYS I WANT
MY BEDROOM TO FEEL

1. _____

2. _____

3. _____

4. _____

5. _____

MY BEDROOM THROUGH MY FIVE SENSES

Sight: _____

_____

_____

Smell: _____

_____

_____

Taste: _____

_____

_____

Touch: _____

_____

_____

Sound: _____

_____

_____

MY BEDROOM'S ZONES

THE BATHROOM

used to approach my bathroom with dread. It was so tiny. It had no storage and felt completely unusable except for the basics. (And by "the basics," I mean the basic human needs we all have.) I have spent the equivalent of college tuition for one semester in trying to find storage-stretching solutions for this micro room.

That is, until I discovered this secret: The smaller the room, the more intentional you have to be about what you use the room for and what you keep in there. If your bathroom is tiny like mine, this is not the place to ignore when it comes to decluttering. Every single item in there must serve a purpose and make your life better.

That's how I want you to approach the bathroom. Ask yourself, *Does everything in here make my life better?* If not, it's time to rethink your space.

DEDICATE

Okay, so hopefully your bathroom isn't one of those multipurpose rooms. (I'm guessing your kids aren't doing their homework in there.) But it's still important to keep it focused. I've had every bathroom size a person could have—my current size being microscopic—and I know without a doubt that, like the kitchen counter, every item needs to earn the right to be in that space.

This is not the place for a lot of extra decorations, knickknacks, or fussiness. If one of your objectives in the bathroom is to keep it—and yourself—as clean as possible, then your goal should be to keep the space as simple as possible.

My bathroom has a few specific purposes I've decided on:

1. taking care of business

2. getting clean

3. caring for myself and my family

4. getting ready

5. relaxing

One of the decisions we made early on in our marriage in order to stay happy was never to be in the bathroom together, under any circumstances, at any point in our lives. Yes, our master bathroom is that small. And we don't do a lot of "extra" stuff in there. It's kind of like the DMV. We get in. We get out.

So I think we are pretty clear on the purpose of this room. But for you? Perhaps your bathroom is a tad bigger than Barbie's dream bathroom. Maybe you have one of those giant master-suite bathrooms big enough for you to host a small book club in it. Whatever you have, make sure you are clear in your mind about the purpose of that room.

Spend a few minutes thinking about what your bathroom is actually used for. Go ahead and list those things at the end of the chapter so you know what your room is dedicated to—and how you can move forward.

It's pretty easy to dedicate a bathroom space. But it's still fun to have a few things that make the bathroom distinctly yours. I love for a bathroom to give a little nod to itself and have some fun. I'm currently considering ordering a sign that says, "No selfies in the bathroom." If I had kids living at home, the sign I would want to have in our kids' bathroom would be, "Potty like a rock star."

But perhaps my favorite way I've dedicated the space in the past was with the cutest hanging quilt of a dog (who looks a lot like our puggle, Jake) wandering in the woods, made by my mom. Above the dog she stitched the words, "It's all about finding the right tree."

If you are a little too grown up for such scatological humor, there are other ways to dedicate the space. Take these examples from the Psalms, for instance:

- "Wash me clean" (51:2 NLT).
- "Cleanse me...and I will be clean; wash me, and I will be whiter than snow" (51:7).
- "He leads me beside still waters. He restores my soul" (23:2-3 ESV).

Make the bathroom your morning inspiration spot. Put up your favorite inspirational scriptures, quotes, and sayings. Let your morning—every morning—start with power.

DECIDE

Now I want you to take a fresh look at your bathroom and decide how to set it up. What would you like to change in your bathroom to make it the mini spa you've always imagined? Since you moved in, you may not have given it a second thought. This, right now, is the time for that second thought.

Are there different ways you could set up the space to make it work for you? What about installing some shelving under the sink in order to hold all your stuff in an organized way? Does the wastebasket make sense where it is, or should you move it to a more convenient location?

Recently, the project manager for our remodel, Nancy, was listening to me moan about how we have no storage in our bathroom. She suggested we create some storage in our bedroom for some of the things we use in the bathroom—such as bulkier items, like towels. We are in the process of looking for either a cabinet or some open shelving for our bedroom, right outside the bathroom, so it doesn't feel so crowded.

These are the greatest priorities for my bathroom:

It needs to be clutter free. There is no room for clutter. None. I need the limited counters and storage space to be the most clutter-free area of my house.

I need my toiletries to be organized and ready for use. The last thing I need first thing in the morning is not to know where the toothpaste is. It is so important that a bathroom has order and process to it. This is critical.

I need it to feel sparkling clean. When we were recently remodeling, I told my contractor that I didn't want anything fancy. I basically wanted to be able to hose down the bathroom like a clean room at a science lab. The kitchen and the bathroom should feel like the cleanest spaces in your house. Last year, when Roger and I had the flu of the century at the same time, I was so grateful that my bathroom was clutter free and easy to keep clean.

Bottom line, I want my bathroom to feel clean, efficient, bright, personal, and refreshing. Here's how I'm working on creating those feelings:

Sight: There is minimal clutter. The room looks clean and inviting. There is great lighting and soothing colors.

Smell: I want this to be the best-smelling room in the house. I want it to smell clean, but not antiseptic. I love a lavender scent when it comes to my soaps and lotions in the bathroom.

Taste: The only taste I want going on in the bathroom is when it comes to my toothpaste, floss, and mouthwash.

Touch: I want fluffy towels and washcloths, and I want to take the chill off in the winter months. I love a thick, fluffy bath mat to step on when I'm getting out of the shower.

Sound: I prefer the sound of running water to anything else in the bathroom, but occasionally I'll listen to music or an audiobook while putting on makeup and doing my hair.

Zones

Following are the zones in the bathroom I concentrate on.

The clean zone. For me, this is the sink, shower, and bath. How do you want this area to function? Are there storage solutions you can implement to make this zone more user friendly? For the shower, consider a corner unit with three shelves to store shampoo, conditioner, and bodywash. If your bathroom is super low on space, you may want to think about dispensers for those products on your shower wall.

You might also want to consider a second curtain rod in your shower. From that, you can hang baskets, a shower pouf, back brush, and loofah. There are also bath trays that allow you to store all your soaps, shampoos, and razors for bath time.

The storage zone. We've installed multiple racks on the back of our door for more towels. If you have a lower shower, you could also consider a shelf right above the shower to store extra towels. And there is always the idea of creating shelving above your toilet (just make sure people can stand up without hitting their heads).

Because we frequently host writers retreats in our mountain home, we've installed three long shelves that each hold three baskets; plus, we have a cabinet below those shelves that can hold three baskets. Each of those baskets is assigned to a person to keep all their "stuff" in. When they prepare to take a shower or get ready for the day, they simply pull out their basket, and everything they need is right there.

The pretty zone. This is for your makeup, hair products, and small appliances. Create a makeup tray that gets pulled out when it's time to get gorgeous. Have a magnifying mirror attached to your bathroom wall to make putting on makeup easier. And if you want low lighting in the bathroom most of the time but need extra light when getting ready, consider a light-up mirror.

The go zone. The most important rule of the "go zone" (besides having a clean toilet) is to never, ever run out of toilet paper. That is why toilet paper storage is my number-one concern in the go zone. There are all sorts of cute cabinets that you can hang over your toilet to keep you supplied in TP. Also check out skinny storage cabinets designed to go between your toilet and the wall, specifically made to hold several rolls of toilet paper.

DECLUTTER

How can such a tiny room attract so much clutter? It's one of the great mysteries of the world. That being said, it is now time to make the hard (and not so hard) decisions about what to keep and what to declutter in the bathroom.

Here are some obvious things to pitch:

- *Anything that smells "off."* I cannot tell you the number of times I've been decluttering with a friend or client and heard, "I bet this is still good." I take a whiff and... *no.* Anything that smells off is bad and should be pitched immediately. (I don't care how much you spent on that contact lens cleaner. How much would you pay not to have an eye infection?)

- *Anything you don't like.* People kept giving me plumeria-scented Bath and Body Works products years ago. The problem? They reminded me of the smell of a certain feminine hygiene product from my teen years. (Sorry to get all graphic on you, but you need to understand why I really didn't want to smell like that.) Instead of giving them away to someone who wasn't deeply scarred by the smell at 17, I kept them in my bathroom for years until I just had to pitch all the bottles.

- *Anything that doesn't work.* I don't know why my immediate thought is to put something in a drawer or under a cabinet if it doesn't work. Since when do electric toothbrushes resurrect themselves? It is time to get it fixed or pitch it.

- *Anything you don't use.* For whom or what are you saving it?

- *Anything that is expired.* And if it's something you use, or something you might need in an emergency, please go buy it.

If you are currently in possession of six different types of conditioner for your curly hair (because, like me, you've tried everything known to womankind in an effort to find something that works to tame those curls), it is now time to use them all up. Or, in my case, it's time to gather up the five that gave me less-than-spectacular results and give them to my daughter, who also possesses curly hair and may have better luck with them than I did—or at least will have more fun playing with them than I did. And let's be crystal clear: This is not about giving other people your junk. My daughter, being curly headed and broke, would love to receive these products. Remember, only give those extras to someone who would be thrilled to receive them.

Think of your bathroom as the best, most exclusive spa. A spa would never hold on to products that don't work or lotions that have gone crusty. They want to give their customers only the best experience with products that are useful and lovely and a space that invites relaxation and restoration. That is what I want you to be thinking of as you declutter your space: *Does this item bring me closer to being at peace?* If not, it's time to get rid of it and create the space you will love to live in.

While decluttering, think of all the spots in your bathroom. I know it's a small room, but it's easy to overlook areas just because "they've always been that way." Look at this list and make sure you've gone through these:

- ☐ shelves
- ☐ medicine cabinet
- ☐ vanity or storage under the sink
- ☐ cabinets and drawers
- ☐ area around bathtub
- ☐ shower shelves
- ☐ floor
- ☐ counter
- ☐ storage bins and baskets
- ☐ linen closet with deep shelves (where things get lost in the back)

- ☐ towel rack
- ☐ behind the door
- ☐ windowsill
- ☐ kids' bath toys

DO YOUR THING

As I'm writing this section, we are in the process of remodeling our bathroom. Let me tell you a few things I've learned in the past few weeks: You can either buy a car or remodel a bathroom. They cost about the same. When Chip and Joanna Gaines talk about how much it costs to redo a bathroom, they are not talking numbers that would apply to someone like me, who is redoing a single bathroom. They are talking about how much it costs them, the people who redo rooms all the time.

It's always going to be more expensive than you originally thought. Always. And there will always be water damage. Always. Just keep that in mind.

Your bathroom is most likely the smallest space in your house. So let me encourage you to have a little fun with this space and make it one of your favorite rooms. Whether you want to go for a spa-like feel or make a splash, spending a little time really thinking through how you want your bathroom to function and feel is the key.

Now that you've decluttered and created some smart storage in the room, it's time to give it some personality.

Update your towels, washcloths, and bath mat. This does not have to be expensive. Our favorite towels are the ones that Costco has carried forever. I'm sure there are other, softer towels out there in the world, but I love that if I accidentally get "hair highlights" (read: red hair dye to cover up the gray) on one of my towels, I can go and replace it without any hassle. I would rather replace a medium-quality towel every couple of years (you should replace towels when they start to lose their absorbency) than spend too much on a towel and try to make it last a decade.

Find a color that will make you happy to look at in the morning. It could be a fresh, white, fluffy towel that wraps you up and makes you feel cozy or a bright pop of color on the wall or shower curtain to really wake you up.

Create a spa set. I love walking into our bathroom and seeing all my favorite lavender products (hand soap, lotion, body mist) on a tray. I can wash my hands, moisturize, give a squirt of my favorite smell, and be on my way. I have all of these products on a little silver tray that is easy to clean and looks amazing. I recommend gathering all your favorites into one pretty spot. Set it up so that the next time you walk into the room, you feel loved and special.

Combat those smells you don't love. Have a way for people to take care of business after taking care of business. Poo-Pourri is a toilet deodorizer that you spray before sitting down. It is a miracle, and I'm grateful that I live in a time where such a product is available. (And yes—they have a lavender spray!) I also have a tub of cleaning wipes (I love Seventh Generation's product that smells like lemongrass or Clorox wipes) for quick cleanups in between real cleanings.

The other fun addition we've recently made to our bathroom is an oil diffuser. I don't plug it in every day, but I love when I've taken a long bath or shower and the oil from the diffuser mixes with the steam of my bathroom. It smells glorious.

Reconsider your shower head. If you are still using the shower head that came with the house, may I gently encourage you to reconsider your life choices? We have a large shower head that helps us make sure we get water on all parts of our body, and it is the best thing ever when it's time to wake up in the morning.

Replace your shower curtain (or at least get a new liner). I think people tend to ignore their shower curtains and liners for far too long. You should be washing that curtain at least once a month—more often if you have a lot of kids. If it's time to spruce up your bathroom, replacing the curtain can give you big impact for a little bit of money.

Something I've learned recently about shower curtains: they come in drastically different sizes. I couldn't figure out why our shower was leaking so much each time we took a shower; a ton of water was getting on the floor. The problem? I had a 65-inch shower curtain for a tub that really needed at least a 72-inch version. We replaced the curtain and liner with new ones that fit, and miraculously, there are no more floods in our bathroom.

Consider lower lighting. Having a dimmer on your lighting in the bathroom can help you achieve the mood you desire. My husband says that while it is an electrical project (and should be done according to exact directions so as to not kill yourself), it is a beginner's electrical project and can be done pretty easily. Yes, you want great lighting for putting on makeup (although, the older I get, the more I appreciate "forgiving" lighting), but when it comes to creating a spa experience, low lighting is a great way to achieve that look.

The other way to get this look (without messing around with wiring) is to place a few candles around the room and turn off the lights. If the thought of having candles around with kids or flammable towels freaks you out, I can tell you we are currently enjoying the LED candles we just purchased. They are remote controlled and can be turned on with just a push of a button. All the atmosphere without any of the wax or cleanup.

Add some music. Complete the spa experience by playing some favorite music. I know that you may be tempted to feature "spa music" with a harp or some other stringed instrument, but I would encourage you to find the music you love and go with that. I like some James Taylor or Rend Collective, or even some Carole King—not your typical spa playlist, but I don't have to worry about any other customers complaining about the music.

This is your private spa. Do what you want.

Make your bathroom a place where you love to spend time—not just a visit to check off each morning. I want you to have a powerful start to your day and go out into the world to do all that God created you to do. Let your bathroom greet you in the morning, empower you, and help you move forward. And when it's time to wind down at night, let your bathroom be the place that automatically brings you to a place of rest and restoration.

MAKE YOUR BATHROOM
WORK FOR YOU

1. Don't keep outdated toiletries. Only hang on to the products you are currently using and loving.

2. Clean out the bathroom cabinets.

3. Maintain surfaces that are clutter free and easy to clean.

4. Minimize paper clutter by frequently recycling any magazines that end up in the bathroom.

5. Avoid storing medication in the bathroom, where steam caused from the shower might damage it.

MY TOP FIVE

THE TOP FIVE USES
OF MY BATHROOM

1. _____

2. _____

3. _____

4. _____

5. _____

THE FIVE WAYS I WANT
MY BATHROOM TO FEEL

1. _____

2. _____

3. _____

4. _____

5. _____

MY BATHROOM THROUGH
MY FIVE SENSES

Sight: _____

_____

_____

Smell: _____

_____

_____

Taste: _____

_____

_____

Touch: _____

_____

_____

Sound: _____

_____

_____

MY BATHROOM'S ZONES

THE OFFICE

'll never forget the day I got an office all to myself.

Being a blended family and having more than the standard number of kids (four) in a smaller-than-some house, our three bedrooms were in constant use. As soon as we got down to one kid in the house, we knew that one of those bedrooms had to be turned into an office.

Sadly, it wasn't destined to be my office.

I told Roger that he should take that office since he was working from home full time (yes, I do deserve a medal of some kind) and that I would continue to write and work on the couch, at the kitchen table, and in my minivan.

And then, glorious day, the last kid moved out. (I've never understood empty nest syndrome. Kids moving out is a sure sign you've done your job as a parent. And if your kids are anything like mine, as long as you have a washer and dryer that don't require quarters, you will never miss your adult children for too long.)

I spent a lot of time fixing up my office—painting the walls, picking out a rug and drapes to hide the carpet stains and wall dents that come with having four teenagers, and making the room my own.

And then, three weeks after I settled into the room, one of the kids needed to move back home for a while, and my cute office became a way station for a kid who needed a soft place to land for a while.

Isn't that how offices go? It's always an "office and" kind of space. But just because you have relatives coming to stay or your office is currently being used to cool some freshly baked cookies doesn't mean your need to get business done no longer exists. You need a place to be organized and creative and to take care of all the tasks that must be done to run a modern family.

No matter if you have an entire room dedicated to your work, hobby, or life management, or if you are operating out of a file box in the corner of your kitchen, you need to make sure you have a space where you can take care of business every single day.

DEDICATE

I'm guessing what you use your office space for and what I do are two completely different things. I am a writer and run a business, but on the side, Roger and I run two different vacation rental properties (one in our main home in San Jose, and one in our mountain home when it's not being used for writer retreats). In addition to that, I need a little space to do the things that we all need to do: plan meals, pay bills, schedule doctor appointments, and just keep up on life.

The top five things I use my office for are business, creating, managing our lives, paying bills, and planning. It is definitely a place where a lot of different activities happen, and that work requires a lot of different tools—like my computer, files, and books.

What are the top five things your office is used for? Go ahead and list them at the end of the chapter so you know what your room is dedicated to before you move forward. And really think through how this room should be dedicated. If it's just the tiniest of spaces in a corner of your kitchen, then it's really important to be strategic and purposeful in dedicating your space.

I've had a variety of signs in this space over the years, but I think my favorite has been (and still is) one that I saw in T.J. Maxx after I had promised myself I wasn't going to buy random signs anymore. I was innocently buying sheets and had just wandered into the sign section when my eye fell on a turquoise and white sign that said, "She's a dreamer, a doer, a thinker. She sees possibility everywhere."

It stopped me in my tracks. I read it, stood there for a moment, and felt a tear welling up in my eye. Yes, right there in front of God and everyone, in the middle of T.J. Maxx. And I figured right then and there that if a sign makes me cry on a Tuesday at 4:00 p.m. in the middle of a department store, it is destined to come home with me.

While I don't know if those words always describe me, they describe the *me* I always want to be. And every morning, when I walk into my office, I'm reminded to be a dreamer, doer, and thinker, and to see possibilities everywhere—and in everyone.

I know that there are a ton of funny signs about work that you may be tempted to put up in your space. Things like, "Better days are ahead. They are called Saturday and Sunday." But I'm going to caution you against that. I want you to enter your work and creative environment with a positive and hope-filled attitude. Words are so powerful—that is why I encourage you to dedicate your space with them. So don't start your work each day with the thought in your head that you hate working and can't wait to be done. Start with the thought that while you are working, you are bringing your best self to your task every single day. If you want to keep your creative soul stirred, find a sign that makes you cry in the middle of a T.J. Maxx.

There was a time that I was working from home at a job that I just hated. My boss wasn't my biggest fan, the work was tedious, and I wasn't very good at it. (It relied on being very detail oriented. Not my strong suit.) During that time I had a little sign with Colossians 3:23-24 written on it:

> Whatever you do, work at it with all your heart, as working for the Lord, not for human masters, since you know that you will receive an inheritance from the Lord as a reward. It is the Lord Christ you are serving.

It was a great reminder that I wasn't just working for my boss, or the company that had hired me, or even just to make money for that week's bills. I was working to honor and please God, even when I didn't feel like it.

DECIDE

For my office space, a few things are important to me.

It needs to be current. I need to have only those projects that are current in my office space. The thing that will make me feel overwhelmed more quickly than anything else is feeling like I have a bunch of "dead" files, projects, and stuff lying around.

If your office feels like an extra room, it's easy to let this become the place of "decide later." And deciding later is the fastest way to get to clutter. In order for me to feel efficient, I don't need to have anything from the past holding me back. I need to be constantly leaning forward and moving myself and my projects toward the finish line.

It needs to be clear. I need a clear surface to work on—not one that is cluttered with papers, Post-its, and to-dos. I need to be able to focus on one project at a time. Too many projects piled on top of each other leave me distracted and not able to focus. Clear surfaces are important to me.

It needs to have great lighting. Lighting had never really been an important factor in my life until I started shooting videos and doing video conferences. And now light is my life. I need to have great lighting so that I'm able to shoot video and read and work without squinting. (Who knew that was a thing?)

As I plan and organize my office, I want the room to feel motivating, efficient, bright, clean, and organized. Here's how I work on creating those feelings:

Sight: There is only one project out at a time. The room looks clean and inviting. There is great lighting and the room is painted with soothing colors. I'm inspired by the artwork and décor I have around the room.

Smell: Like all my rooms, I want this one to smell fresh and clean. I lived in Japan for a while, and they have honeysuckle that grows like weeds there in their parks and public spaces. I love the smell of that plant, and it makes me feel alive. That is the scent I choose for my office space. When I want to be productive, I light the honeysuckle candle on my desk and get to work.

Taste: Again, not a room with a lot of tasting going on. However, this is the room where I consume the most coffee and water throughout the day. I've learned that having a coffee cup warmer (my Mr. Coffee one was affordable) and a coaster for water makes my day more hydrated and productive.

Touch: I have two important "feels" in this room, and they are both chairs. I have my comfy chair for reading and creating videos (it is a purple velvet chair, much like the couch on the cover of my book *Clutter Free*), and then I have my office chair. I spent more money on my office chair than I have on most other pieces of furniture because it's where I spend most of my time working. I've done the research on a good office chair that has great back support (something that becomes more important the more, well…wisdom…you gain in this life). A good throw blanket is important to me in this space as well. I have one that is cat and dog friendly (since they spend a lot of time fighting over my lap in this space).

Sound: I have a set of good speakers in this room. I also like to have good acoustic music playing in the background while I'm working. (I can't concentrate on work while listening to the lyrics of my fave songs from the '80s.)

Now it's time to think through and dream about *your* space. How do you want your office to feel? Brainstorm five words to describe your office using the list at the end of the chapter.

Zones

Your office space is going to look nothing like mine. But we all need a place to read, work, and store information. Think through exactly what your needs are and start to dream of the space that you will use and love. This will help you create the zones in your office. Following are some of the zones in my office.

The reading zone. My office is where I do most of my reading and keep the lion's share of the books in my house. (My goal when it comes to books is to keep only the ones I am reading, have a plan to read, need for work reference, or are among my top 50 books of all time. And yes, I have a list.) I have my purple chair to read in, my bookcase, and a great light to read by.

If you are a big reader like I am, think through your reading space. If you don't have room for all the books you'd love to keep, consider purchasing an e-reader or a subscription to Audible. If a book is story driven (memoirs or fiction), I prefer an e-book or audiobook. For years I didn't read much fiction, but I have rediscovered a love for it as I frequently make the three-hour journey between our mountain retreat and our home. If a book is nonfiction, I buy the physical book. I want to be able to refer back to it, mark up the pages, and use Post-its so I can get the most out of it.

The work zone. For me, this is where all the magic happens. This area is the top of my desk, where I have my computer, files that I'm working on, pens, notepads, my planner, and more. If a project is happening, it is most likely happening on top of my desk. This is an important space for me to keep clear and organized. I want to be able to show up in the morning and feel like I can sit down and create—not have to excavate.

Be intentional about your work zone. Since mine involves flat surfaces, I work hard not to pile things on there. I save ten minutes at the end of each day to file, put away, and clear off paperwork and tools in order to take better care of myself the next morning.

The retrieval zone. I'm guessing there are a few documents you need to be able to have access to in order to keep life running. We'll look more specifically at those as you begin to declutter.

DECLUTTER

If clutter is indecision, then there is no area of the house that can bring so much clutter as the office space. The office is where decisions go to die. Plus, this room is the biggest magnet for "I'll put it here for now." But in your office, you want only current projects that need your attention so that you can deal with those and move on with your life.

Let's start by digging into your paperwork. I've looked over others' lists of what should be kept in a "filing system" (I prefer to call it a "retrieval system" so I'm never putting anything in there that I'm not planning on accessing), and I am always amazed at the amount of stuff we're told we should keep.

For example, many sources tell you to hang on to old bank statements. Really? Twenty years ago it was important for my mom to keep all of her bank statements, but that is not the case anymore. My bank gives me access to my recent statements online. Unless you have a reason to go back and look at bank statements, you probably don't need to keep all that. We have switched to paperless statements and have done just fine without that paper coming into our house and taking up permanent residence in a filing cabinet.

I promise, you will never need to retrieve your bank statements from five years ago. (And if you absolutely do because of something weird and wild happening, you can order them through the bank for a small fee). Nor will you ever need to refer to outdated insurance cards again. Whenever you're getting ready to file a piece of paper, ask yourself two questions:

1. *Will I ever need to refer to this again?*

2. *Can I easily find this information somewhere else?*

If your answer to the first is no and the second is yes, you can pitch that piece of paper.

And I know what you're asking yourself. *But what if I need them?* I like to think about it this way: How much would you pay to have your whole house decluttered? Five hundred dollars? A thousand? More? (A whole lot more?) Now, what if you got rid of everything that you "might need someday"? How many of those things would you end up needing to buy again? One? Two?

It's the same with paperwork. Yes, you might get rid of a paper or two that maybe, someday, you will need to track down again. In the meantime, you will have saved yourself from going through the same hundred (thousand?) papers over and over again. Yes, keep the deed to the gold mine your grandpappy left you. But the pay stub from 1997? It's time to let that go to the great recycling center in the sky.

Now, it is possible for me to track down my birth certificate, but it's a pain. So the last time I had to order one, I ordered a few extra copies to have on hand. Those came in handy when I got married, needed a passport, etc.

This was something I also learned when my dad passed away: order—and keep—extra copies of the death certificate. Some places will need for you to present a certified copy of a death certificate, while some will be okay with a digital copy. All I know is that when you are offered the chance to purchase a certified copy of the death certificate, get five. You'll thank me later.

There are a few types of paperwork you will want to keep on hand and be able to retrieve at a moment's notice. Keep anything related to your insurance, real estate, retirement, medical records (if your doctor doesn't keep them for you), and any current loans you may have. But get rid of the paperwork you'll never refer to again. Don't let the junk mail anywhere near your filing system. Get rid of the old projects you're never going to complete—you've moved on to bigger and better things. Toss those old receipts, except the ones you need for taxes, and don't worry about the car loan company or mortgage company not keeping a record of your payments. As long as you are paying from an account with a bank or credit union, there will be a record on the sending end of that transaction. (Of course, if a transaction is still pending, you'll want to keep the paperwork until it's gone through.)

One of the areas that is hardest for me to declutter in the office area is the ghosts of jobs (or passions) past. When I was in my early thirties, I was a sales rep for a number of different gift lines. I sold everything from stuffed animals to candles to wind chimes to glass figurines. Yes—I sold clutter for a living.

I would go into stores and bring catalogs of my different lines for the stores' buyers to see and order from. I stored these catalogs in giant leather binders. I think now about how today's sales reps are just carting around a five-pound laptop, and I want to break into speeches about how, in my day, I had to carry my catalogs around in leather binders, uphill both ways, in the snow…but I digress.

I loved that job and felt I was very good at it. It worked great with having kids in elementary school—I was able to be home with them most afternoons—and I loved the people I worked with, as well as my clients.

But then I went through a bout of situational depression. My marriage was falling apart. I started to stay home instead of going out on calls to work with clients, and then I started hiding from clients. I had the most understanding, tenderhearted boss on the planet, but neither of us could avoid the fact that I wasn't doing my job. I resigned, with his offer that when I started to feel better, he would do everything he could to make space on the team for me again.

After several months of depression and years of trying to save my marriage, the relationship came to an end. I ended up moving about two hours from San Jose to my parents' home in the Sacramento area.

And guess what moved with me? Those black leather binders.

I just couldn't get rid of them. I longed for a day when I could go back to my life before divorce—the life where I was working at a job I enjoyed, living in a home I'd helped create, sending my kids to a school they loved. And for some strange reason, those binders became the thing that I just could not let go of. To me, they represented the life I wanted to go back to. In my new town, while I was grateful for my parents and their generosity, I didn't have the life I wanted. I wanted to go back to San Jose, where I had friends, a church, a job. And those black binders represented all of that.

Isn't it crazy how we give inanimate objects so much power in our lives? In the office, it is so easy to try to hold on to past lives. Maybe a project you were passionate about no longer fits you or your life. The problem? You spent so much time, energy, and money on this particular project that it feels like a huge waste to let it go.

If you are facing a situation like that, here are a few ideas to help you let go of that object from a past life:

Pray about it. I have done this with many of my items that were special to me and hard to give away. I pray that I have the strength to make the right decision. If I can't get myself to give it away just yet, I pray that God will give me the strength in the future.

Find someone who could really use it. It is an order of magnitude easier to give something away when I know that someone else is desperate for it. About eight years ago, I had amassed a huge collection of scrapbooking paper. (I had promised myself that I would do scrapbooks for each kid. And then the internet came along with the cloud and photo storage and saved me from scrapbooking.) The problem? I had picked out just the right paper for each kid and hated to give up something into which I'd put so much time and energy.

So I did something brilliant without knowing it: I gave away a small part of my collection. One of my friends is an elementary school teacher who is always doing creative projects with her kids. I asked her if she wanted some paper, and when she said yes, I handed over about 5 percent of my collection.

She was thrilled. Ecstatic, really. After seeing her reaction, I had no doubt that my paper was in much better hands with her than me.

Trust God it will get to the right person. Some of us who deal with clutter want to make sure that our stuff we are giving away will get into the hands of the "right" person. So we hold on to our stuff until that "right" person presents themselves.

But that can keep us locked to our clutter for much longer than necessary. Donating that item and trusting that God can get it into the right hands is a freeing, beautiful way to live.

As you declutter, keep an eye on this list of spaces and make sure you've hit all the areas of your office:

- ☐ top of desk
- ☐ desk drawers
- ☐ bookcase
- ☐ filing cabinet
- ☐ stackable filing trays
- ☐ markers, pens, and pencils

☐ paperwork to be shredded

☐ cubbies (window seat, extra storage containers, etc.)

☐ memo or bulletin board

☐ floor

☐ extra furniture that's become a paperwork catchall

☐ electronic storage

☐ photos and memorabilia

☐ anything hanging on the door or stuffed behind it

☐ catchall baskets (holding random electronics, old mail, old paperwork)

☐ old books

☐ overflow from other rooms shoved here (slow cooker, fondue pot, etc.)

☐ business inventory

DO YOUR THING

Your office space needs to be as amazing as you are. Now that you have done a ton of decluttering, it's time to make this space productive and fun.

Have some visual prompts. Maybe it's a corkboard to keep ideas for projects on or a whiteboard to keep a running list of all the steps for a project. Having a place to visually focus on your work is welcome and motivating in your office space.

Create a command center. For some people, their command center is in their kitchen. For me, it's in my office. I want to be able to see everything I need to refer to at one time. Consider framing out a section of one wall to hold your calendar, whiteboard, vertical files for projects, or whatever will help you keep your important stuff in front of you.

Think about the colors in this space when you work. Do you want pops of color to wake you up in the morning, or do you need a more peaceful place to get work done? I settled on warm gray walls with pops of turquoise, and it feels like home to me.

Get a bookcase. I know that you've been decluttering your books, and I also know that it feels painful each time you do it. But if you are a big reader, get a great bookcase that not only stores your how-to guides and Jane Austen collection, but can also feature some of your favorite framed photos and precious objects. While you're at it, make sure you've gotten rid of books you won't read again. There's no reason to keep books around as trophies. We get it—you read.

Consider some new filing solutions. If your work space is more of a "mobile office" (like a corner of the kitchen and the breakfast table after you've swept the Cheerios off of it), then being able to complete tasks and stash them when you are done is super important.

For the years that I lived with a nomadic office, I had fabric-covered file boxes I stored in a hutch in the living room. I brought them out to the kitchen table whenever it was time for me to work. The issue with this is that you have to be willing to put the boxes away at the end of your work time—otherwise, they become part of the clutter that gets easier and easier to ignore.

If this is your situation, you may want to consider a few different solutions.

- IKEA has the RÅSKOG rolling utility cart that is perfect for storing files, office supplies, and more. It can be rolled out when you are rolling up your sleeves and getting ready for work, and it can be tucked into a corner or a closet when it's time to go watch a little Netflix. And at less than $30, it's a fun, affordable solution.

- A portable printer can be tucked into a drawer and set up each time you need it. Since our society's printing needs are becoming less and less, this small amount of inconvenience may be worth it.

- If you have a closet or piece of furniture where you can store files or supplies, shoeboxes in different colors can help you quickly recognize what you are looking for and help make cleanup faster as well.

I'm writing this from a hotel room in Utah, where I've just attended a convention with members of my family. Normally, after an event, I would put everything in my suitcase to bring home and "sort out later" (you know, pile up on my counter and eventually, two years later, throw away in a decluttering whirlwind). But not with my newly acquired clutter-free mind-set. Now I'm spending 15 minutes this morning to sort through everything I picked up—the flyers and instructional sheets, workbooks and programs—and tossing what I don't need and organizing what I do need. This is going to make tonight's unpacking a breeze, and I won't clutter up my office with unnecessary stuff.

I want to do this because I'm living a clutter-free life. But I'm also doing this because I want to come home and keep the rooms nice that I've worked so hard to clean and organize. Besides unpacking, all I have to do when I get to my office and start working tomorrow is go through any mail or packages that have come in and cut some more roses to put in the Mason jar that is on my bookshelf. And those? Are the chores I like to come home to after a vacation.

MAKE YOUR OFFICE WORK FOR YOU

1. Maintain an up-to-date filing system.

2. Have space to create, dream, and breathe.

3. Keep surfaces clutter free and easy to clean.

4. If your income is dependent on the work you do in your home office, invest in sturdy and practical office furniture.

5. Keep a recycling bin nearby so that you can easily and quickly get rid of any paper waste.

MY TOP FIVE

THE TOP FIVE USES
OF MY OFFICE

1. _____

2. _____

3. _____

4. _____

5. _____

THE FIVE WAYS I WANT
MY OFFICE TO FEEL

1. _____

2. _____

3. _____

4. _____

5. _____

MY OFFICE THROUGH
MY FIVE SENSES

Sight: _____

_____

_____

Smell: _____

_____

_____

Taste: _____

_____

_____

Touch: _____

_____

_____

Sound: _____

_____

_____

MY OFFICE'S ZONES

THE OTHER SPACE

H
ere is where we enter the land of the lost when it comes to our homes and clutter.

By "other spaces," we're talking garages and basements, the room that was left behind when your kid moved out, the "guest" bedroom (that hasn't seen a guest in years because of all the extra stuff in the closet), your husband's man cave, your "she shed," and the craft or hobby area that may or may not look like a team of elves came in, created Christmas, and abandoned the project when it came time to clean up.

My major "other space" is the garage—otherwise known as the place where hope goes to die. As long as I've been on my clutter-free journey, the garage is the place that has given me the most trouble. Here in California, I would say that only half of my neighbors use their garage as a spot to park their cars. My friends and I tend to have smaller houses (not smaller house payments—just smaller houses), so the garage is used for all manner of storage. The problem is that we're storing indecision instead of things we actually need to run our lives.

I'm guessing your "other space" is one of the harder areas to keep decluttered in your house. It is the place where you put everything that overwhelms you until you "have time" to deal with it. (And when does that time ever magically appear?)

You may have multiple "other spaces" throughout your home. Please just take it one space at a time. It would be completely overwhelming to take on all the extra spaces of your home as one giant decluttering project. As you go through that special room, work the plan for that one room, and when it is good enough, move on to the next "other space." Remember, just take it one space at a time. You've lived with the chaos. You can live with it a little longer. Working the system will help you not just "clean a room" for a week but make changes for a lifetime.

DEDICATE

Of all the spaces, this one may be the most difficult to dedicate. The problem? It's probably the area that most desperately needs to be dedicated to a specific purpose, as it's likely being used for too many purposes.

Sewing or craft room. If your "other space" is a sewing or craft room, it's important that it doesn't also become an "everything else we can't figure out where to put" room. I love the idea of hanging a sign that says "_____'s Craft Corner" so that you (and other family members) don't get any crazy ideas about using the room to store out-of-season gear or Pokémon card collections.

I am not much of a crafter, but I have lived with one for almost half my life. (My mom is an award-winning quilter. Those creative genes skipped a generation.) I've picked up a few tips and tricks from her.

- For no one else (except possibly a teacher) is it more important to clear out old projects and resources. This will be your fastest way to keep on top of your projects and craft a space in which you want to create.

- Have a simple way to keep all your tools at hand—whether it's a spray-painted pegboard, a shelf with bins, or an old dresser.

- Whatever you do, focus on creativity and function in this space.

Guest room. I think this is where you can have a lot of fun. My sister-in-love, Debbie, is an amazing hostess. We have stayed at her home a lot while visiting family in Georgia. I always feel like I'm putting people out when I stay in their homes—I understand the work that goes into getting your place ready when you have people come and visit.

But with Debbie, I know I'm welcome. There is a chalkboard sign in our room—see how welcome I feel? I call it "our room"—that says "Welcome, Roger and Kathi." That is a room lovingly dedicated for guests.

Garage. Our garage can't be just for the car. My family needs to use that space for a lot of different things. We store business inventory, garden supplies, emergency supplies, and tools. It also functions as an extra pantry and freezer.

Since this space has to have so many uses, instead of going in there and just putting everything in boxes that we pile in one big heap, we've needed to create zones for the garage.

We've already talked about the importance of zones, and we'll get into more specifics later in this chapter. But zones are especially important in your "other spaces." Make sure that your tools (like crafting supplies) are not commingling with your high school yearbooks. If you need to keep different items in the room, set up an area for each category and then label those areas.

In our garage, we have big signs in each of the different zones so we don't shove things that don't belong into that area and create clutter. You would never store the graham crackers in your bedroom closet. Make it equally ridiculous to store your pruning shears in the "Emergency Supply" area. Setting up your extra space like a large kindergarten room, with clearly marked areas, bins with labels, and so much intentionality that if someone called you when you were out of town and asked you where your glue gun is, you could tell them? Well, friend, that's living the dream.

But (and this is a huge warning) the worst thing you can do is go into that room and start setting up bins for all the things. It's important to walk through the four steps first. You can set up the bins and do all the labeling *after* you've decluttered all you can. That's the key—to only organize and categorize what you will actually use and need.

For me, my ever-present "other space" is my garage, so I will be using that for my example here. The top five things I use the room for are parking our car, storing, providing extra pantry space, keeping tools, and housing our gardening equipment. What's your top-five list? Go ahead and list the uses of your space at the end of the chapter so you know what your room is dedicated to.

DECIDE

In my garage, a few things are important:

It needs to have plenty of storage. The storage I'm speaking of here isn't a couple dozen boxes of decisions waiting to be made. Most of this is inventory and equipment and props for my ministry. It all has to be organized and easy to find, but the items are pretty bulky and need to be contained. Roger and I spent a lot of time finding the right racks and cabinets that would help us store what we need to store while still giving us quick access to anything we need to grab.

It needs to be accessible. It's not enough to store things out there. Everything has to be accessible so I can actually use the stuff. I employ a gardening cart and toolbox for accomplishing tasks around the house. If my supplies are tucked away, getting small tasks and jobs done quickly becomes very difficult.

It needs to have great lighting. I'm becoming more and more convinced that great lighting in every room is essential. Having adequate lighting isn't just a convenience—it's a safety issue.

I want this room to feel organized, clear, bright, clean, and safe. Here's how I'm working to create those feelings:

Sight: There is little I love more than walking into my garage and knowing exactly where everything is. It feels like a superpower. Having a clean space that is free from visual distraction is my own little piece of paradise when it comes to my garage.

Smell: Like the bathroom, my biggest goal is for this area to smell like nothing. For years when my kids were growing up, the biggest smell I had to contend with was Jeremy's hockey equipment and uniform. (Hockey: the smelliest of all sports.) I used a lot of laundry detergent and a lot of "de-funking" methods to keep that from killing us all as we walked into the garage. (Do yourself a favor—encourage your kids to join the chess team.)

Taste: Nothing to taste in this space. But I do keep a pantry in the garage and have had to invest in some great storage containers so that the city mice don't end up eating all our Costco cereal, brown rice, and dog food. The rest of my pantry is contained in old wooden bookshelves, where I store bottles, jars, and cans.

Touch: Feel is not such an important need out in the garage, but one of the things I have invested in for all garage and backyard activities is great gloves. It is so much easier to get down and dirty when I have a great pair of gloves covering my hands. (I'll admit it—I hate getting dirty.)

Sound: Because I spend time in the garage organizing, packing up boxes for events, and taking inventory, I love playing music or audiobooks out there to make the time go faster. I have a Bose speaker that can connect to my phone and keep me company.

Now it's time to think through and dream about *your* space. What do you need to do to make it work and feel like it's all yours? Brainstorm some ideas in the space at the end of the chapter.

Zones

What are the zones in your extra space? Here are just a few examples from my garage:

The storage zone. Yes, we have a lot of storage in the garage (but every year I'm trying to get that to be a smaller and smaller amount). We store tools for household repairs, paint, little-used appliances (like our fondue pot and raclette set), serving dishes, holiday décor, and camping equipment.

One of the best things I've discovered for keeping the storage zone organized is Duck Pack and Track. This is a system where you put labels on your storage boxes, scan the QR code on the label, and input (by voice or text) what is in the box. So when it comes time to look for your backup Instant Pot (because shouldn't everyone have a backup Instant Pot?), you can just search the Pack and Track app on your phone, and it will tell you exactly where it is and what box it's in. Genius.

The gardening zone. I am a light gardener. I just have a back patio to use, so it's not like I'm out there hoeing rows, but I do need a space to keep tools, extra pots, soil and additives to keep my container garden going and growing.

This is also the area where I've had to realize that just because I bought something for the garden five years ago (when I was more "into it") doesn't mean I need to keep it forever. I have decided that I travel too much to actually keep up with a tomato garden—plus, nothing will make me angrier than seeing a squirrel taking a bite out of one of my tomatoes on the vine and then leaving it there, ruined. My love affair with homegrown tomatoes is officially over. But I can plant herbs and pretty much leave them alone for the entire growing period, except when I want to clip them. So herb pots stay, tomato pots go.

The fix-it zone. We need to keep a small area of the garage dedicated to tools and household fix-it supplies. We have made space by getting rid of some of our bigger tools because, well, we live in a town house and don't need that much. Since Roger is a fix-it guy for the twenty-first century (in other words, he fixes computers), and home maintenance will never be my sweet spot, we leave larger repairs to the professionals.

DECLUTTER

Find something to hold on to tightly. I know the thought of decluttering your garage, basement, attic, or any of the "other spaces" in which boxes and bags have accumulated is enough to make you want to find a fainting couch and have the lady's maid go fetch the smelling salts. (Come to think of it, if you had a lady's maid, all that clutter would be her problem.)

Don't start with the hard decisions, like figuring out what to do with your grandmother's china. Get rid of the obvious things—the empty boxes, broken items that are never going to get repaired, duplicates (you don't need a backup vacuum), anything with water damage, paint that no longer matches any of your rooms, and other people's stuff. (Give the owners a time limit to pick up their items. After that date, everything gets donated.)

As you're decluttering, be sure to check all these spaces:

- ☐ storage closet under the stairs
- ☐ window seat
- ☐ mudroom, hall closet, coat closet, entryway
- ☐ storage shed, barn, outbuildings
- ☐ toolboxes
- ☐ medicine cabinets
- ☐ pet areas and supplies
- ☐ baby items no longer in use (like strollers)
- ☐ bags, including reusable shopping bags
- ☐ memory boxes and children's artwork
- ☐ mementos and antiques
- ☐ purse
- ☐ inside of the car
- ☐ side pockets of recliners
- ☐ holiday storage
- ☐ homeschool room
- ☐ attic or cellar, crawl spaces
- ☐ patio, porch, sunroom
- ☐ exercise room and equipment
- ☐ toy boxes, toy room
- ☐ deep-freeze appliance or extra freezer
- ☐ storm shelter, bomb shelter, panic room

DO YOUR THING

When it comes to your "other space," function over form is the name of the game. That doesn't mean you can't enjoy being in the space, but I've got to be honest: When it comes to my garage, I want to get in, find what I'm looking for, and get back to my project as quickly as possible.

So while you are reading through these tips, remember: while all those color-coordinated garages on Pinterest may be adorable, wouldn't you prefer *adorable* for the house and *easy to navigate* for your "other spaces"?

Be ruthless about what you keep. I know that you already decluttered in the last step, but keep asking yourself if you need what you're storing. There is no use organizing clutter. Get rid of it once and for all and then you won't need to spend the next decade reorganizing it every time you clean the basement.

Think vertical. In the garage, your walls and ceiling can be your most valuable assets. We have a shelf that hangs down from our ceiling in the garage that holds light items we use semi-regularly (suitcases, coolers, the cat carrier, etc.). Those are items that take up a lot of square footage, but they don't have to be on the floor.

On the walls, use pegboards to hang tools, gardening equipment, and supplies. That's a great way to make everything visible and accessible. If there is one thing I know about us cluttered people, it's that we like to be able to see things and not have them hidden away in cabinets. This is a great way to be able to stay organized and see what we need at the same time.

Keep it clean. One of the reasons we all tend to avoid these extra spaces is that they can get so dingy and dirty that we'd just rather ignore them. I have found that it's so important not only to put things back when I'm done with them (so my basement doesn't become a jumbled mess once again), but also to clean as I go. Dust that box lid, clean up that spill. Have systems set up so that you can easily get rid of items you don't want or no longer need (recycling, garbage, or stuff to give away).

Repurpose. In the first home I owned, the previous owners had ripped out their old cabinets to install new ones. They put the old cabinets in the garage. Genius. This was my favorite garage storage system ever.

If you don't happen to be in the middle of ripping up your kitchen, go with my second favorite idea: white, lockable cabinets. These are cheap and easily available at any home-improvement store. You could line one side of your garage with these cabinets and the other with a couple of racks with see-through tubs (using the Duck Pack and Track labels, of course)—and have all the storage you will ever need.

When it comes to other spaces, remember to give yourself grace. Sometimes it takes years to build up that much clutter. Often, some of our most emotional clutter decisions are sitting in the garage or attic. (That hand-stitched quilt your grandmother made that matches nothing else you own? Not an easy decision!)

If you're stuck on a particular area or item, it's okay to move on to another space. Don't try to start with family heirlooms like Great-Grandma's World War II–era china. Instead, work through the camping bin you haven't touched since you moved from another state.

It won't happen overnight, but I promise that if you use the steps in this book, you'll have functional spaces that will work for you and your family. The more those areas get freed up, the more you'll be freed up to do what God created you to do.

MAKE YOUR OTHER SPACE
WORK FOR YOU

1. Have a system for knowing where items are stored.

2. Stop storing indecision and nonsense.

3. Maintain clear zones for each category of storage.

4. If a particular item induces guilt whenever you see it, the best way to get rid of the guilt is to get rid of the item.

5. Find a way to display those items you treasure, such as mementos and heirlooms, rather than keeping them stored in a box.

MY TOP FIVE

THE TOP FIVE USES
OF MY OTHER SPACE

1. _____

2. _____

3. _____

4. _____

5. _____

THE FIVE WAYS I WANT
MY OTHER SPACE TO FEEL

1. _____

2. _____

3. _____

4. _____

5. _____

MY OTHER SPACE THROUGH
MY FIVE SENSES

Sight: _____

_____

_____

Smell: _____

_____

_____

Taste: _____

_____

_____

Touch: _____

_____

_____

Sound: _____

_____

_____

MY OTHER SPACE'S ZONES

LIVING CLUTTER FREE WITH KIDS

One of the most frequent questions I get through the Clutter Free Academy is, "What about my kids' clutter?" Conflict over clutter can damage any relationship over time, but it's especially crucial to navigate this issue carefully with your kids. What you teach them right now will influence their lifestyles as adults.

As parents, we want to empower our children to have the life skills they need to succeed. Below are four ways we can help our children learn how to live a clutter-free life.[5]

Schedule short decluttering times.

Saying, "We are going to declutter for 15 minutes," instead of, "Let's clean this room!" makes decluttering bearable for anyone, young or old. We're more likely to focus better if we only have to declutter for 15 minutes (time boxing). If your kids are young, set a timer and make a game of it. For example, challenge your five-year-old to clean out one drawer in five minutes. I don't expect anyone to spend hours at a time decluttering. (In fact, I absolutely discourage it). For children especially, decluttering works best in small, manageable sessions.

By the way, I want to differentiate between cleaning and decluttering. Cleaning means putting things away, mopping, vacuuming, and dusting. Decluttering means getting rid of stuff you don't love, don't use, or wouldn't buy again. While they are two different tasks, they are both important for your children to learn and perform—but keep the tasks separate so they can focus their attention on one or the other.

Teach by example.

It's been said that in raising kids, more is caught than taught. They tend to learn more from what we do than what we say.

Like us, kids aren't born knowing how to declutter. The best way to teach them is to work side by side with them to show them the same decluttering systems you've been learning. Make sure they have the tools they need—three totes, two bags—so that they have a system in place to declutter. Go through the steps one by one: what to give away, what to put away, and what to take back to a different room. Any trash or items to recycle go into the bags.

Have a fun celebration when you empty the contents of the totes and bags into their rightful places. It doesn't have to be a big deal—a sticker, a high five, or a "Yay! You did it!" all work great.

Focus on one tiny space at a time.

Trying to declutter a large space is even more overwhelming for kids than it is for adults. Choose the smallest area possible, such as a drawer or shelf (space boxing) and set the timer. Even better—let your kids choose which area is the most problematic for them. If they already see the value of decluttering, then you've won half the battle.

Divide up the closet into small sections, sort one drawer, go through one toy box at a time. Decluttering is a gradual process. Their space didn't get cluttered in a day! A consistent habit of setting a timer to declutter a small space will result in big changes.

Help them maintain their space.

To help keep the rooms of your house organized and tidy, teach your child routines. Set times during the day when they put away school papers, toys, backpacks, clothes, and anything else out of place. Even five minutes in the morning and five minutes in the evening will work wonders.

To help with motivation, make a timed game out of it. They'll be motivated even more by getting consistent rewards each week for working through their routines. Before you know it, picking up their things will become a habit.

Parent–child dynamics are already challenging enough. Reducing clutter conflict can go a long way to improving the relationship. When it comes to clutter, our relationship with our kids is so important. When we come alongside them and give them the tools and skills they need to create a clutter-free home, we free them up to be who God made them to be.

And let's be clear: If we can gain some more sanity in our days by teaching them to declutter their own spaces, all the better!

USE IT UP, WEAR IT OUT, MAKE IT DO, OR DO WITHOUT

know certain people like to complain about the fact that they had to walk uphill to school both ways as kids. (Not me, of course. I rode my rainbow Schwinn bike uphill both ways.) But back in the day, our grandmothers really did have it rough. During World War II, everything from socks to sugar to meat to (gasp!) coffee was rationed. Which meant everyone had to do without—and do without a *lot*.

Americans were urged to eat mostly fruits and vegetables (which were too hard to transport overseas to the armed forces) and go without meat and flour ("Meatless Tuesdays" and "Wheatless Wednesdays") so those precious resources could be saved for our fighting men. Slogans such as "Food will win the war" reminded people why they were rationing.

And while I'm not about to give up my mocha gelato (even in the name of decluttering), I do think we have something to learn from this. One of World War II's most popular mottos was "Use it up, wear it out, make it do, or do without." And a tiny part of me thinks we should bring that back.

USE IT UP

In January, I gave myself a challenge: Go six months without buying any toiletries. No cosmetics, no hair products, no bath products, no toothpaste, no toothbrushes. Now, before you assume that I had an aggressive disregard for personal hygiene, I want to assure you that smelling good is an important priority in my life, and I am very fond of my teeth. My problem was that my bathroom clutter had taken on a life of its own.

I had hair products coming out of my follicles and enough cosmetics, nail polishes, and skin buffers to start my own little MAC counter. I did a little archaeological digging through all my products and tried to uncover the reason why I'm addicted to buying them. In the process, I learned a few things about myself.

- I am a hair product junkie. I will buy anything that anyone recommends to control my frizzy red hair. Apparently money (and storage space) is no object.

- I'm addicted to shopping at Costco. I don't buy one tube of toothpaste; I buy six. Even if I just bought six the last time I went to Costco four weeks ago.

- I don't know how to throw away mostly empty bottles. And I don't know how to use the last little bit to drain the bottles. I just hang on to those mostly empty bottles forever, like high school participation trophies.

- I don't know how to throw away products that cause severe allergic reactions.

- I don't know how to throw away gifts that someone gave me even if the smell makes me slightly queasy.

- I'm not aware of what I already have, so when I'm at the store, I buy more just in case.

- I've never met a hotel shampoo, conditioner, lotion, or mouthwash I didn't want to bring home with me.

All these clutter traps led to a situation that was really and truly out of control. So I put myself on a six-month product-buying sabbatical. Here were my rules:

1. I was going to use up all the products in my house until they were gone or the six months were up—whichever came first.

2. If I didn't want to use a certain product (I'm looking at you, almond body butter), then I needed to throw it away.

3. Only once I was completely out of a product could I go buy some more. That meant if I was going to buy shampoo, I first had to use up any old, almost-empty bottles, off-brand shampoos, and tiny bottles I'd grabbed from hotels. If I wasn't going to use them, I needed to dump them or pass them on.

It was a simple challenge, but it wasn't easy. Whenever I'd get my hair done, my stylist had a new product to try. When I traveled, I had to make sure that I had all my products with me—no emergency trips to Target to get hair spray.

But once those six months were up, my stash of products was much smaller, and I only had items that I truly used and loved. Plus, I didn't spend one dime on products during that time. (Yes, I still got my hair cut and spent money to maintain my redhead status; there are some things on which a girl cannot compromise.)

THE "USE IT UP" CHALLENGE

Once a year, try a "use it up" challenge in your bathroom. Don't buy any new products until you use up what you already have. This helps with "someday, maybe" thinking. Like, "Someday, maybe I will use that Korean facial mask that looks like a panda, so I better just hang on to it." Or, "Someday, maybe I will have oily skin again like I did in my teens, so I better hold on to this astringent." That is exactly the kind of thinking that gets us into the cluttered situations in which we find ourselves.

As you start to use up your favorite products (shampoo, eyeliner, bodywash, foundation, etc.) and it comes time to replace them, shop your house instead of Target. Use that bodywash you got at last year's Christmas gift exchange at work. Then use the one that you used to like before you found this new scent you love. Use up all the bodywash, and when there is no more to be found in any of your stashes, you now have permission to go to Target and buy a bottle of any bodywash your little heart desires.

Now, if you are cleaning out your stash and a bottle is "off" (smells bad, looks crusty, etc.), do *not* use that bottle of bodywash. In fact, if you don't *like* that bottle of peppermint bodywash, don't use it. But don't put it back in your stash. It is time to either dump the bottle, rinse it out, and recycle the plastic, or give it to someone who would love it. But the most important part is to make a decision about that bottle.

At the end of your time (and if you've been doing the challenge for a month and realize you need to go longer, do it!), you will have a lot less clutter and a lot more free space. Plus, now that you really know what you want, you will only buy and use products you love. How great and spa-like is that?

People like me who struggle with clutter tend to be ones who love to try new products, always looking for the one thing that will make their teeth brighter, their hair shinier, and their floors brighter. We end up having dozens of journals with writing only on the first page, bottles of product half-full, and magazines half-read. We find ourselves buying new books while the old ones remain unread on our shelves.

Maybe the stash threatening to take over your life isn't in the bathroom, but in your craft space. Of all the people I know, crafters may be the most natural stockpilers. My mom is a quilter, and the stockpile of material she owns would put many small, independent quilt stores to shame.

The other natural stockpilers? Teachers. And who could blame them? When most teachers are paying for their own materials, room decorations, and art supplies, it's no wonder they don't want to give up any of their hard-earned stash.

It's great to have options on hand, but look for ways to use up the materials you have before buying more. And when it is time to buy something, have a plan to use that item—all of it!

Clearing Out the Kitchen

The main area of the house where "use it up" can go a long way is in the kitchen. If we can learn to apply the "use it up" principle in this area of the house, it will go a long way to saving us time, space, energy, and money. Before developing a clutter-free mind-set, I would have been mortified to tell you how much food I shopped for, paid for, lugged home, let sit in my fridge for a couple of weeks, and then, sadly, threw away. I always had the best of intentions (especially for that broccoli and zucchini), but it was a crime how much of that food eventually went to waste.

And it wasn't just the perishables in my fridge. My pantry was a mess of cans and bags I never touched. If I was planning on buying one can of garbanzo beans to make homemade hummus, I would naturally buy a case of beans at Costco, assuming that I would use them up eventually. The problem? I found out I like my hummus made with dried beans, so I was stuck with seven cans of beans I would probably never use.

Feel free to stock up on the items you know you go through. Buy that case of stewed tomatoes if you use a can a week. Stockpiling sensibly saves you money, but stockpiling items you might want to use someday is never a good plan. If you end up throwing out the food because you haven't used it up in a timely manner, you've wasted time, space, energy, and money.

I've learned to take inventory of what I have in our fridge, pantry, and especially the freezer. I keep a mental "watch list" of fruits, vegetables, breads, milk products, and meats that are quickest to go bad. In my fridge I have a small shelf holding cheese that has been opened, butter sticks that are cut in half, salami that is about to expire, and salad toppings (shredded carrots, chopped celery, sliced cucumbers) that need to be eaten. This "use it up" shelf is a reminder that these things need to be eaten first so that we don't waste food and money. Why eat cheese that will expire in three months when you have some that will expire in three weeks?

As you're applying the "use it up" principle in your kitchen, go through your fridge and pantry to see what needs to be used up. Look at the foods that will need to be tossed in the next few days if you don't use them. Instead of defrosting chicken for tomorrow's dinner, combine the two containers of leftover chicken. If you have the choice between eating those veggies you cut up a couple of days ago or buying new veggies at the store, use the ones you already spent time preparing. Make a salad with the big tub of veggies that are going to go bad in the next few days. Take that leftover hamburger meat and turn that salad into a taco salad with tortilla chips.

Here are some other ways you can use what you've already got:

YOYO. At least once a week we have a YOYO night (You're on Your Own) when, instead of fixing dinner from scratch, we eat up what's already in the fridge.

Lunches. Lunches are an excellent way of managing leftovers. As you are putting away dinner leftovers, figure out whose lunch they will be tomorrow.

Make a plan before you store. Before you pack up that leftover chicken and put it in the fridge to be used "later," make a plan for how and when you're going to use it. Once leftovers go into the fridge, they are easily forgotten.

Get creative with leftovers. Some of our favorite meals are made from leftovers. When I roast a chicken, I always save the leftovers for Greek yogurt chicken salad, one of our favorite healthy meals. Monday night we eat a delicious roast chicken, and then on Wednesday we have our chicken salad with crackers for lunch. Planning ahead means that none of the chicken gets wasted.

Have a "use it up" week once a month. If you tend to be a stockpiler (and most of us who struggle with clutter are), you probably could live very nicely off your stockpile for a while. Once a month, just buy the basics at the store (milk, bread, produce) and see what you can use up in your stockpile for the week.

Find some recipes. Some websites, like www.supercook.com, will suggest recipes based on the ingredients you have on hand.

Shop your pantry before you shop your store. We've all done it—arrived at the store and then thought to ourselves, *Do we have milk? I can't remember. I'll pick up some just in case...* And that "just in case" jug of milk is now the fifth gallon of milk in your fridge. Before you go to the store, double-check what you have at your house so you're not spending your valuable grocery dollars on stuff you already have.

Yesterday we had some friends over for dinner. I challenged myself to see how much of the meal I could make from ingredients I had on hand instead of buying all new ingredients at the store. Since the weather was beautiful, we decided to barbecue. After surveying the pantry, I decided we would have Roger's family-famous grilled hamburgers, macaroni salad, and watermelon. We had everything on hand except for the buns (which I had all the ingredients to make, but I decided that $2.99 was a fair trade-off for not having to spend two hours in the kitchen), the watermelon, and the celery and green onions for the macaroni salad.

MICHELE CUSHATT'S GREEK YOGURT CHICKEN SALAD

Season and cook three large chicken breasts in 1–2 tablespoons of olive oil until done, then dice and put into a large bowl. Squeeze the juice of one large lemon over the chicken. Add nonfat, plain Greek yogurt and a tablespoon or two of honey or agave to taste. Add a chopped tart apple, dried cranberries, toasted almonds, and green onions (optional). Serve with crackers or lettuce cups...or eat it with a spoon right out of the bowl.

BEWARE OF AUTO-SHIP

Delivery services make it so easy to have supplies shipped automatically to your front door. It's so convenient! That is, until one day you go into the garage and see that you have six cases of kitty litter.

I would only suggest auto-ship for nonperishables, and only if you are willing to closely monitor what is being shipped and when. We use it for our pet needs (since they eat the same diet every day) but have had to adjust our delivery dates and amounts over time.

Another category that has worked out well for us when it comes to auto-shipping is our vitamins, since I can count exactly how many pills we will take each day.

If your auto-ship orders have left you with a stockpile, most services allow you to skip a month (or two) and pick up where you left off.

WEAR IT OUT

In a study of 32 families in the Los Angeles area, researchers noted over and over again that families would purchase a new item but fail to get rid of the item they were replacing.[6] Since the old item was still in working order, they hung on to it, intending to sell it on Craigslist or at a garage sale. Meanwhile, they kept cramming more and more into every room of the house.

We have become a nation of replacers, not repairers. When our shoes get scuffed, we toss them out instead of getting them repaired (or even shining them). Instead of sewing on a stray button, we buy a new shirt. My daughter had a college friend who threw away a pair of running shoes because she didn't know you could buy replacement shoelaces.

Instead of replacing items, what if we took the time to refurbish them? What if we were to purchase something with the thought in mind that we would only replace it when it was beyond repair? What if we made purchases for the long haul? Instead of buying patterned dishes (and growing tired of them after a couple of years), buy plain ones you can mix and match with what you already have. Buy furniture with the knowledge that it's going to acquire a few scratches and dents along the way.

I want my house to look not only "lived in," but "loved in." And that means resisting the urge to replace stuff all the time. I know I'm going to start sounding like your old crotchety grandfather right now, but keeping your old things is a lot cheaper than buying new ones. I know my dad used to always talk to me about things like "proper car maintenance" and "regular oil changes" and "not pressing so hard on the brake just because you think you saw a squirrel." It may have sounded like *blah, blah, blah* when I was younger, but now I know the wisdom in his advice. If my car—my totally-paid-for car—lasts a year longer than it would have if I hadn't maintained it, all those oil changes would be worth the trouble. If we take care of our things, we not only save the trouble and cost of buying new ones, but we have nicer things to use when we need them.

Here are some simple hacks to help make the items you have last:

1. Hang-dry your nice sweaters and dresses so they don't get worn out from constant heating and cooling in the dryer.

2. Only use a dime-sized amount of shampoo and bodywash (it says so on the bottle!) and use a sponge or washcloth to rub it in.

3. Only let your kids wear their nice shoes to school and church. Get a cheap pair of flip-flops or sneakers for them to wear at home or in the mud.

4. Set the table with mismatched china or pieces from multiple sets for special occasions. It will look "shabby chic" (which is code for "totally cool").

I want my house to look not only "lived in," but "loved in."

MAKE IT DO

If there is any concept that goes against Pinterest board or Amazon Prime living, it is "making do." And what does it mean to make do? It means that when you are faced with a situation where you "need" to buy something (which has always been my go-to answer) you stop, take a second, and ask yourself, *Is there a way to accomplish what I want to do without buying something or bringing something new into our house?*

When I used to hear, "Oh, we can make do with…" it represented a poverty mentality to me. I thought it meant not having needed resources and getting by with second best. But now that I've gone through the hard work of decluttering my house, the last thing I want to do is add more clutter.

One of the reasons we bring new things into our home is because we're not exactly sure about what we already have. And the reason for that? Probably because we've got too much stuff. We've all been there: We go out and get that cute new shirt for a special event, bring it home, and feel all fab in it…and then realize (or worse, our spouses point out to us) that the shirt looks exactly like one we already have.

If I asked you right now to think of something cute to put on your nightstand, would you think of pulling something from another room in the house, or would you think about going out and buying something new? For years, my first instinct would have been to go to T.J. Maxx or Target to go buy something cute. But now my mind goes to the question, *Is there a way to accomplish what I want to do without buying something or bringing something new into our house?*

Here are some of the things I've "shoplifted" from my own home:

- I brought baskets out of hiding. I had loads of baskets in my closet that were too cute to keep hidden. I spray-painted them white and now use them in the kitchen, my office, and our living room.

- I had a silver tray I never used as part of a tea set. I now use the tray on my nightstand to hold my glass of water and a tiny vase with a rose in it.

- The glass containers that used to hold my kitchen staples (flour, sugar, etc.) are now in our laundry area holding our laundry powder, OxiClean, and Method pods.

- I took an old tissue holder, and it is now our dryer sheet dispenser.

I continually ask myself, *What can I use to get this job done that I already have?* One of my favorite examples of this concept is from the book *The Complete Tightwad Gazette* by Amy Dacyczyn. In this book, Amy shares how to make a postage scale with items you already have around your house.

> To make a postal scale you need a 12-inch ruler, a pencil and five quarters. Put the ruler on the pencil so that it is centered over the 6-inch mark, or in the center. Place the

quarters (which weigh 1 oz.) on the 3-inch mark. Center
your sealed envelope on the 9-inch mark. If the quarters
don't move, you know your letter is under 1 oz.[7]

What she and I really love about this idea is that when you are done,
the ruler and pencil go back into your desk drawer, the quarters go into
your change jar, and there is no weird scale sitting on your desk, taking up room.

One of the "make do" areas that I have had to make huge changes in
is the kitchen. For so long I have approached cooking as an exercise in
uninhibited creativity. I figure that if I'm going to the trouble of cooking, I should get to make what I want. I enjoy cooking from scratch
when I make the time, so one of my favorite activities has been thumb-
ing through recipes in my favorite cookbooks or on Pinterest, creating
a list of ingredients, heading to the store to get my groceries, and coming home to make the magic happen.

While this approach led to a bunch of great meals, it also led to a
bunch of food languishing in our fridge and pantry, eventually to be
thrown out. I experienced a paradigm shift when I realized I could be
even more creative if I took the ingredients I already have on hand and
create a great meal out of those instead of making another trip to the store.

I love how smart I feel when I "make do" with what I have. Since
those of us who tend toward clutter also over-shop at the grocery store
(it has a lot to do with our "just in case" thinking), this is a great way
to force ourselves to be creative when it comes to cooking and "using
it up."

And it's not just in the pantry that our kitchens get out of control.
We can also learn to make do in the area of kitchen gadgets. There are
a million gadgets that will make a job easier. The problem? They only
make that one job easier. (I call these "one-hit wonders.") Let's take the
corn cob remover as an example (who knew this was a thing?). This is a
contraption that looks a lot like a yellow hand pump, and you put the
cooked ear of corn in the cylinder. Push the arm down, and the blades
inside the cylinder will strip off the kernels of corn effortlessly.

Now, if you are someone who needs to take the kernels off an ear of corn on a weekly basis, this may be a great purchase for you (and operators are standing by to take your order), but most of us do not have such extreme shucking needs. So when I am tempted to buy one, I ask myself, *What do I already own that I could use to strip my corn?*

Would you believe you can use a Bundt pan? After you've shucked the corn, removing as much silk as possible, put the stem of the corn in the hole of the Bundt pan to hold the corn steady. Take your knife and cut along the base of the cob to remove the kernels. Once all the kernels are removed, use the back of the knife to scrape along the cob to get as much of the corn juice as possible. The brilliant thing about this method? All the kernels and juice are collected into the Bundt pan. No mess.

But what I love even more is that I already have a Bundt pan sitting in my kitchen. If I'm smart, I don't need a drawer full of tools that only have one use and get dug out once or twice a year. I can be creative, find other solutions, and not let marketers tell me that I need a different tool for every little thing in life.

So now, instead of running to Bed Bath and Beyond to buy a heart-shaped cupcake pan in order to make a Valentine's treat for your daughter's fifth grade class, you can Google how to make heart-shaped cupcakes with the pan you have. (Pro tip: Just stick a marble between the cupcake liner and the pan to bend the cupcake into a heart shape as it bakes.) Or, instead of making heart cupcakes, you can make round cupcakes that the kids will devour in less than 90 seconds. Those will do just fine.

DO WITHOUT

My husband and I are taking "do without" to the extreme. We are about to go down to one car. My minivan (which is fifteen years old and has been on the "make it last" plan for the past six years) recently got back from our trusty auto mechanic, who told my husband, "I've known you for a long time, so it's even harder to give you the bad news, but it's the transmission. Your van only has so many more miles to go." Fixing the transmission on a 15-year-old car is like buying curtains for a hotel room—it's a bad investment. We knew this day would come, so about five years ago we started saving up money for a new car.

But as the end drew nearer and nearer, the idea of replacing the car became less and less appealing. I work from home 90 percent of the time. The other 10 percent is mostly airplane travel. I do very little driving. And since Roger works from home two days a week and doesn't work on weekends, there is a car available to me four days a week.

So now I'm purposely not driving my minivan in order to make it last as long as possible. When it finally dies, will I survive without a car? Yes. Will I decide after six months that adding a second car back into our lives is necessary for the health of our marriage? Perhaps. But we are doing something we've never done before: We're asking ourselves the question, *Can we do without?*

Our culture is not set up for the mind-set of "do without." It's about as un-American as you can get. You don't even have to read magazines or watch TV to get bombarded with advertisements for all the things you didn't know you actually totally need. So in a culture that encourages you to buy more—now!—and can always distract you with a shiny new item, it's time to start thinking through when you can postpone the purchase of a book—or a car, or a house, or a new pair of shoes.

Roger and I love a show called *America's Test Kitchen*. I mean *love*. It's a PBS show in which cooks demonstrate different recipes they've tested multiple times in order to get it just right. With cooking being one of our few hobbies, we love to jump into the kitchen and re-create some of those recipes.

That's not the part of the show that gets us into trouble.

There is another segment called "Equipment Review" in which a man named Adam shares the results of testing a dozen ice cream scoops, or eighteen food processors, or nine skillets. And I'll be honest, there have been many times when, at the end of this particular segment, I have had my laptop out and been logged in to my Amazon account, ready to order a paring knife I didn't know I needed until I saw these reviews. In our home, it's the most expensive show to watch.

Why do I justify the expense? Because we actually use, on a regular basis, all the tools we've bought after watching "Equipment Review."

But I've learned to show extreme restraint. The show has featured so many great products I want to try. An electric waffle maker? I've lived for the past 20 years without one, but wouldn't it be nice to wake up in the morning to hot waffles? An offset spatula? That would be great for cake decorating! A pitmasterIQ barbecue controller? How have I lived this long without it?

The problem with each of these devices? I would have to be living a completely different life in order to use each of these. I would never wake up to the smell of waffles because I would be the one making them. (And just for the two of us? Pancakes seem a whole lot easier.) And while an offset spatula would be great for cake decorating, decorating cakes is not something that brings me a lot of joy. It would probably get used twice a year, if at all. And I live in a townhouse where charcoal grilling is not forbidden, but it's definitely not enjoyed by our neighbors who don't get to eat our roasted pork but have to deal with the smoke. So in these cases, while tempted, it is just better to do without.

In the past, I would have come up with a dozen reasons why I needed that electric citrus juicer and the set of brioche pans. Then they would have sat around my house for five or six years before I decided that I just needed to make room and sent them off to the donation center. I would rather donate my money to causes I care about than a kitchen store.

The great thing about using it up, wearing it out, making it do, or doing without? It's a simple principle to put into use once you get the mind-set. If your first instinct is no longer to run to Target every five minutes, your decluttering efforts will become much easier.

I'm not suggesting that you always have to employ MacGyver-like tactics when you need something new, but I do know that most of us could save a lot of time decluttering (and money too) if we became intentional about using what we already have.

A FINAL WORD

One of my favorite ways to procrastinate on my writing is by watching the History Channel. (I can convince myself that at least it's educational and a step up from watching anything with the word *housewives* in it.) My all-time favorite show is *American Pickers*. I could watch Mike and Frank go through people's "treasures" all day. In fact, today I spent much of my day doing just that while working on other projects. (Okay, if we are going to be 100 percent accurate, I may have been looking for projects to do so I could keep watching.)

When Roger came downstairs after a several-hour flu-induced nap, he said, "I can't believe you are still watching that!" (He would like for me to point out that he had absolutely zero accusation in his voice. He just knows I'm not normally into all-day TV marathons.)

"I know! I don't know why I'm so addicted to this show," I replied sheepishly.

"Oh, I know," Roger said. "It combines your two favorite topics: clutter and story."

He had me. That's exactly it. I can't help but be compelled by the mounds of clutter that so many people have in their homes, garages, outbuildings, and—in more than a few cases—school buses parked in their backyards. I'm fascinated by the draw to have so much *stuff* in their lives, especially when that stuff ends up choking out the rest of life: the relationships, the activities, the finances that most of the rest of the world values.

But then there are the collectors who have the story of how their collections got started: how they would hang out with their dads after school and work on cars or go to the movies with their brothers, and everything they collected brought back those memories.

And what makes me so happy, what just thrills my heart, is when people are ready to let go of the stuff. They get older and wiser and realize, truly, that their relationships are not built in the stuff, but are built with the people with whom they made the memories.

That was my turning point, and it is my hope for you. That the stuff you are surrounded by can be scaled back not only to reveal the home you've always dreamed of, but the life you were always intended to live.

Our homes are just a resting, refueling, and restoration point for the rest of our lives. Yes—our homes can be a big part of our lives, but they are not the whole thing. My dream is that you will stop being a servant to your home and that your home will, eventually, serve you and the people you love.

NOTES

AT PEACE WITH YOUR HOME

1. Decluttr, "Survey Finds 54 Percent of Americans Are Overwhelmed with Clutter and Don't Know What to Do with It," PR Newswire, *Cision*, January 13, 2015, http://www.prnewswire.com/news-releases/survey-finds-54-percent-of-americans-are-overwhelmed-with-clutter-and-dont-know-what-to-do-with-it-300019518.html.

STEP 1: DEDICATE

2. C.S. Lewis, *The Last Battle* (New York: HarperCollins, 2002), 228.

3. J.R.R. Tolkien, *The Fellowship of the Ring* (New York: Del Rey, 2012), 252.

THE KITCHEN

4. Julia Child to Avis DeVoto, Paris, January 5, 1953, *As Always, Julia*, ed. Joan Reardon (New York: Houghton Mifflin Harcourt, 2010), 31.

LIVING CLUTTER FREE WITH KIDS

5. Thanks to one of my team members and fellow empty-nester mom, Lyneta Smith, for contributing to this chapter.

USE IT UP, WEAR IT OUT, MAKE IT DO, OR DO WITHOUT

6. Jeanne E. Arnold et al., *Life at Home in the Twenty-First Century: 32 Families Open Their Doors* (Los Angeles, CA: Cotsen Institute of Archaeology Press, 2012), 28.

7. Amy Dacyczyn, *The Complete Tightwad Gazette: Promoting Thrift as a Viable Alternative Lifestyle* (New York: Random House, 1998), 114-115.

Acknowledgments

While writing a book can feel like a lonely process, a book is never written alone. I'm grateful to my team—the people who love, support, and often drag me across the finish line of each book.

Thank you to my entire ministry team, specifically the Rock Stars—Angela Bouma, Tonya Kubo, Cheri Gregory, Shantell Brightman, Tiffany Baker, and, most especially, the wonderful Lyneta Smith. None of this would be possible without all of you.

To the Clutter Free Academy community: Thank you for being the test group of every single idea in this book. You've made a huge difference in the lives of thousands of people—giving overwhelmed people hope that clutter doesn't have to run their lives. Your stories and faithfulness are world changing, and I'm so proud of each and every one of you.

Thank you to our reader team. You made this book better by your loving (and honest) feedback.

Kathleen Kerr. Every author should get to work with you at least once in their life. Thank you for pulling out the best in me.

Rachelle Gardner. Thank you for your continued support and belief. I am so, so grateful.

To my mom, Connie Richerson, who provides so much practical help to keep our lives running: Roger and I (and Jake the puggle) are so grateful.

And finally, thank you, Roger. For loving our team well. For loving our family well. For loving me well. Your powerful combination of being strategic in business and loving others well has made an impact on the lives of countless people, and I'm so grateful that I get to be your partner in all things. Shut the door, baby.

KATHI LiPP's
clutter free academy ●●●

The Clutter Free Academy began with a long road of conquering clutter and all the baggage it carried for Kathi Lipp. As the author of *Clutter Free: Quick and Easy Steps to Simplifying your Space*, Kathi found her passion—helping others become the world changers they are meant to be by conquering the clutter that stands in their way.

The Clutter Free Academy exists to teach people why they have clutter, how to get rid of it, and how to never let it take over their emotional, physical, and spiritual life again. With books, large events, podcasts, webinars, eCourses, and one-on-one coaching, the Clutter Free Academy provides hope and healing through real-life tools that can be implemented personally and in households, classrooms, corporations, and ministries alike.

For more information, contact us at
info@clutterfreeacademy.com

and subscribe to the podcast at
www.clutterfreeacademy.com

About the Author

Kathi Lipp inspires thousands of women each year to strip down their expectations and live with real purpose. With humor and wisdom, she offers hope paired with practical steps to live with meaning.

Kathi is the author or coauthor of 17 books, including *Clutter Free*, *The Get Yourself Organized Project*, *The Husband Project*, and *Overwhelmed*. She is the host of *The Clutter Free Academy* podcast and speaks at conferences across the United States. She also runs the Facebook group Clutter Free Academy, where thousands of women (and a few brave guys) support each other in living a clutter-free life.

She has become well respected on the topic of clutter from a biblical perspective (who knew there was such a thing?). She is a national speaker and is often featured on Focus on the Family, MOPS International, Crosswalk.com, Girlfriends in God, and Proverbs 31 Ministries, as well as a number of other media outlets around the country. She has been named "Best of Broadcast" on Focus on the Family twice.

Kathi and her husband, Roger, are the parents of four young adults in San Jose, California. When she's not dating her husband or hanging out with her puggle, Jake, she is speaking at retreats, conferences, and women's events across the country. Visit her at www.kathilipp.com

Let Kathi Lipp and Cheri Gregory show you five surprising reasons why you become stressed, why social media solutions don't often work, and how you can finally create a plan that works for you. As you identify your underlying hurts, uncover hope, and embrace practical healing, you'll become equipped to...

- trade the to-do list that controls you for a calendar that allows space in your life
- decide whose feedback to forget and whose input to invite
- replace fear of the future with peace in the present

You can simplify and savor your life—guilt free! Tasks and relationships may overwhelm you now, but God can help you overcome with grace.

More to Enjoy
from Kathi Lipp

101 Simple Ways to Show Your Husband You Love Him

21 Ways to Connect with Your Kids

The Christmas Project Planner

Clutter Free

Get Yourself Organized for Christmas

The Get Yourself Organized Project

Happy Habits for Every Couple

The Husband Project

The Me Project

The Mom Project

You Don't Have to Try So Hard

To learn more about Harvest House books and
to read sample chapters, visit our website:

www.harvesthousepublishers.com

HARVEST HOUSE PUBLISHERS
EUGENE, OREGON